AF342231

Redeemed from the Curse

Redeemed from the Curse

Paul's Understanding of the Law and Gentiles in the
Light of Hellenistic Judaism

HYUN-GWANG KIM

WIPF & STOCK · Eugene, Oregon

REDEEMED FROM THE CURSE
Paul's Understanding of the Law and Gentiles in the Light of Hellenistic Judaism

Wipf & Stock
An Imprint of Wipf and Stock Publishers
199 W. 8th Ave., Suite 3
Eugene, OR 97401

www.wipfandstock.com

PAPERBACK ISBN: 978-1-6667-6055-2
HARDCOVER ISBN: 978-1-6667-6056-9
EBOOK ISBN: 978-1-6667-6057-6

05/31/23

For my wife, Sung-Hee, and daughters, Yoon-Young and Min-Young.

Contents

Acknowledgments

THIS BOOK IS BASED on my doctoral dissertation at the Southern Baptist Theological Seminary, Louisville, Kentucky, USA. It was a great privilege for me to study and write about Paul under the guidance of wonderful scholars. I would like to thank my *Doktorvater*, Dr. Mark A. Seifrid, for his grace, wisdom, and careful guidance. My committee members, Dr. Thomas R. Schreiner and Dr. John B. Polhill, were gentle and supportive during every stage of my dissertation. I also appreciate Dr. Timo Laato, the external reader, for his insightful comments on my work. The continuing encouragement of Dr. Jeffrey A. D. Weima, my former advisor at Calvin Theological Seminary, was invaluable.

I could take action to publish this book while I stayed at Western Theological Seminary for a sabbatical year. I am grateful for the gracious support and friendship of President Felix Theonugraha, Dean and Vice President of Academic Affairs Kristen Deede Johnson, Professor of New Testament Emeritus Dr. Robert Van Voorst, and many other members of the Western community. Without a sabbatical leave, this book would not be possible due to my teaching and administrative duties in Korea. I appreciate President Uoo-Chung Kang and my colleagues at Korean Bible University for graciously providing this sabbatical.

My wife, Sung-Hee Lee, and our two daughters, Yoon-Young and Min-Young, have been a continuing source of strength and joy for me. The prayers of my parents, Dong-Sik Kim and Keum-Sun Han, and parents-in-law, Rev. Eui-Suk Lee and Keum-Soon Kim (deceased 2009), have been positively answered for me by the grace of God. I sincerely thank them all. I pray that this book may be used for the glory of God and to help the church to understand Paul and his letters better.

List of Abbreviations

AB	The Anchor Bible
ABR	*Australian Biblical Review*
Abr.	Philo *De Abrahamo* (On Abraham)
Ag.	*Ap.* Josephus *Against Apion*
AM	*Adorare Mente*
Ant.	Josephus *Jewish Antiquities*
ANTC	Abingdon New Testament Commentary
Bar	Baruch
BBR	*Bulletin for Biblical Research*
BECNT	Baker Exegetical Commentary on the New Testament
BNTC	Black's New Testament Commentary
BZ	*Biblische Zeitschrift*
CBCNEB	The Cambridge Bible Commentary on the New English Bible
CBQ	*Catholic Biblical Quarterly*
CC	Concordia Commentary
CNT	Companions to the New Testament
EBC	Expositor's Bible Commentary
EBTC	Evangelical Biblical Theology Commentary
EKKNT	Evanglisch-Katholischer Kommentar zum Neuen Testament
ERT	*Evangelical Review of Theology*
GSC	Geneva Series Commentary
HNTC	Harper's New Testament Commentaries

ICC	International Critical Commentary
IVPNTCS	IVP New Testament Commentary Series
JBL	*Journal of Biblical Literature*
JETS	*Journal of the Evangelical Theological Society*
JJS	*Journal of Jewish Studies*
JQR	*The Jewish Quarterly Review*
JRE	*Journal of Religious Ethics*
JSJ	*Journal for the Study of Judaism in the Persian, Hellenistic and Roman Period*
JSNT	*Journal for the Study of the New Testament*
JSNTSup	Journal for the Study of the New Testament Supplement Series
JSP	*Journal for the Study of the Pseudepigrapha*
KEK	Kritisch-exegetischer Kommentar über das Neue Testament
LCL	Loeb Classical Library
LNTS	Library of New Testament Studies
Mos. (Moses)	Philo *De vita Mosis* (Philo *On the Life of Moses*)
NAC	The New American Commentary
NASB	New American Standard Bible
NCBC	The New Century Bible Commentary
NIB	The New Interpreter's Bible
NICNT	New International Commentary on the New Testament
NIVAC	The NIV Application Commentary
NIGTC	The New International Greek Testament Commentary
NovT	*Novum Testamentum*
NSBT	New Studies in Biblical Theology
NTL	The New Testament Library
NTS	*New Testament Studies*
Opif	*Philo De Opificio Mundi*
OTP	*The Old Testament Pseudepigrapha*
PCNT	Paideia Commentary on the New Testament
PNTC	The Pillar New Testament Commentary

Pss. Sol.	*Psalms of Solomon*
SBJT	*The Southern Baptist Journal of Theology*
SBLSP	*Society of Biblical Literature Seminar Papers*
SEÅ	*Svensk exegetisk årsbok*
Sib. Or.	*Sibylline Oracles*
Sir	Sirach
SP	Sacra Pagina
SR	*Studies in Religion/Sciences religieuses*
SPhiloA	*The Studia Philonica Annual*
THKNT	Theologischer Handkommentar zum Neuen Testament
TNTC	Tyndale New Testament Commentaries
TynBul	*Tyndale Bulletin*
WBC	Word Biblical Commentary
Wis	Wisdom of Solomon
WTJ	*Westminster Theological Journal*
WUNT	Wissenschaftliche Untersuchungen zum Neuen Testament
ZECNT	Zondervan Exegetical Commentary on the New Testament

CHAPTER 1

Introduction

ARE THE GENTILES UNDER the law in Paul? Paul states in Rom 2:14 that gentiles do not have the law. He emphasizes gentiles' being without the law twice in Rom 2:14: (1) ἔθνη τὰ μὴ νόμον ἔχοντα, (2) οὗτοι νόμον μὴ ἔχοντες. It is apparent that gentiles did not receive the law of Moses on Mount Sinai. When Paul enumerates in Rom 9:4 the privileges of the people of Israel, he points out God's giving of the law to the Israelites: "who are Israelites, to whom belongs the adoption as sons, and the glory and the covenants and the *giving of the Law* (ἡ νομοθεσία) and the temple service and the promises."(NASB) According to Rom 2:14 and 9:4, Paul is not likely to say that gentiles are under the law.[1]

The Problem

Is it legitimate then to conclude that gentiles are not under the law in Paul? The answer is not as simple as one might first imagine. Let's take Gal 4:4 as an example. Paul describes in this verse the incarnation of Christ with regard to the law. Christ was "born *under the law* (γενόμενον ὑπὸ νόμον)." When Paul identifies Christ as the one who came to be under the law, does Paul mean that Christ was born as *a Jew* in light of Rom 2:14 and 9:4? If that is the case, the following verse must be interpreted as saying that Christ was born as *a Jew* to redeem only the *Jewish people*, because Paul

---

1. See also Rom 3:2 and 1 Cor 9:21.

says in Gal 4:5 that Christ was *born under the law* "in order to redeem *those who were under the law*."[2]

In a similar vein, if gentiles do not have the law (Rom 2:14), is it wrong to say that *gentiles*, as well as Jews, "were kept in custody *under the law*, being shut up to the faith which was later to be revealed" (Gal 3:23 NASB)? Does this verse refer only to the Jews being confined under the law?

Is it also unthinkable to say that the law was the *gentiles'* παιδαγωγός until Christ, so that *gentiles* may be justified by faith (Gal 3:24)? Or otherwise, does Paul restrict the law's function as παιδαγωγός only to the Jewish people because they are only the people of the law?

Galatians 3:13–14 could be provided as an even more complicated statement of Paul on the law and gentiles. Gal 3:13–14 reads:

> Christ redeemed *us* (ἡμᾶς) from the curse of the law, having become a curse for *us* (ἡμῶν)—for it is written, "CURSED IS EVERYONE WHO HANGS ON A TREE"— in order that in Christ Jesus the blessing of Abraham might come to the Gentiles, so that *we* would receive (λάβωμεν) the promise of the Spirit through faith. (NASB)

Given the fact that gentiles do not have the law of Moses, could it be considered correct to understand that Christ redeemed *gentiles* from the *curse of the Law*, having become a curse for *gentiles*? Or is it preferable to say that Paul refers to Jewish Christians exclusively with the first personal pronoun "us" in this passage, due to the fact that the Jews are the only people under the law of Moses? To raise the fundamental question again, what have gentiles to do with the Mosaic law in Paul's theology?

This question could be answered with the following three possible responses: (1) Paul understands that gentiles are not under the law because they do not have the law. Only the Jews have something to do with the law. (2) Conversely, and although it appears to be ironic, Paul puts gentiles under the law even though he acknowledges that they do not have the law. There might be some reasons and theoretical background for Paul to express the relationship between the law and the gentiles in this way. (3) He reveals his confusion concerning the relationship between the law and gentiles by saying gentiles are under the law in one place and then saying gentiles are without the law in another place. I shall delve into the relationship between the law and gentiles in Paul's theology with these three possible answers in mind.

---

2. Scripture quotations are my translation, unless noted otherwise.

Significance

To inquire whether or not Paul understands gentiles to be under the law is important, because how we understand the relationship between the law and gentiles determines our comprehension of Paul's soteriology. Our understanding of God's economy for the gentiles' salvation is radically dependent on how we identify, for instance, the first person plural ἡμᾶς in Gal 3:13. In this regard, T. L. Donaldson's statement is worthy of citing:

> If, as many argue, this is an inclusive group of Jewish and Gentile Christians, then there is only one linking step between "cross" and "Gentiles": the (universally) redemptive effect of Christ's becoming a curse "for us (all)" on the cross. But if, as many others contend, those who are redeemed from the curse of the law are Jewish Christians exclusively, then an intermediate step is assumed: the redemption of Israel as a prerequisite for or condition of (cf. ἵνα; v. 14) the blessing of the Gentiles.[3]

If ἡμᾶς in verse 13 is interpreted as referring to the Jews exclusively, the meaning of verses 13 and 14 can be rendered such that Christ redeemed the Jews first from the curse of the Mosaic law, so that in Christ Jesus the blessing of Abraham might also come to the gentiles. In this view, the Jews' redemption from the curse can be understood as a prerequisite for the gentiles' salvation.

The purpose of Christ's incarnation can also be understood differently as we have already considered above, depending on one's comprehension of the relationship between the law and gentiles. If one holds that Paul refers to the Jewish people exclusively with "those who were under the law" in Gal 4:5, the purpose of God's sending his Son in Gal 4:4–5 can be understood as God sending his Son to *redeem the Jews*. This study will eventually help us to better understand Paul's soteriology for the gentiles.

In addition, many controversial Pauline texts, which could not yield a consensus among Pauline scholars, will be more clearly and correctly understood by the proper comprehension of Paul's view on the law and gentiles. Thus, the inquiry of this book will contribute to the scholarly advancement in understanding Paul and his letters.

3. Donaldson, "'Curse of the Law' and the Inclusion of the Gentiles," 94.

Background

I have been interested in the relationship between Jews and gentiles in Paul's theology. As a result, I have conducted exegetical studies regarding 1 Thess 2:13–16, Eph 2:11–22, and Gal 2:1–10 as they relate to this issue. As I attempted to understand the relationship between Jews and gentiles, I believed that I had to deal with the relationship between the Jewish law and gentiles. Paul defines gentiles as people "not having the law" (Rom 2:14). It seemed to me, however, that Paul places gentiles under the curse of the law in Gal 3:10, 4:4, and 4:5. In addition, it was interesting to find out that many prominent Pauline scholars do not agree about the identity of those who are under the curse of the law in Gal 3:13. In this respect, I felt that the relationship between the law and gentiles in Paul's theology requires further clarification.

Thesis

The thesis of this book is as follows. Paul understands that gentiles are under the law as well, even though the law was not given to them by Moses on Mount Sinai. In Paul's theology, paradoxically, gentiles, who do not have the law, are not exempt from being under the law and its curse. This idea can be observed in the Pauline corpus, including Rom 2:12–16, Gal 3:13–14, 23–24; 4:3–6. Consequently, Christ redeemed gentiles as well as Jews from the curse of the law by becoming a curse not only for the Jews but also for the gentiles in his substitutionary and representative death on the cross. There are not two stages of salvation between Jews and gentiles, i.e., first stage: Jews' redemption from the curse of the law, second stage: Abraham's blessing for gentiles. Paul never informs us about the idea that the Jews' redemption from the curse of the law is the prerequisite for the following gentile redemption. That he understands gentiles to be under the law is not entirely unique, because a similar notion can be found in the literature of Hellenistic Judaism, including Sirach. Paul's regarding gentiles as under the law can be understood in light of his understanding of God, who created the universe and reveals his wisdom by both his creation (natural law) and the Mosaic law (written law) as we can see in Rom 1–2 and Hellenistic Judaism. Therefore, the notion of gentiles' being under the law, which they never possessed, does not represent any theological problem or illogical thinking on Paul's part.[4] He might have used that notion to explain his gospel effectively to the Hellenized world, which maintains the concept of natural law and

---

4. Contra Räisänen, *Paul and the Law*, 9–15, 18–23.

written law.[5] In Paul's theology, Christ died on the tree for *gentiles*, as well as Jews, to redeem not only Jews but also gentiles from the *curse of the law*.

Method

Those who are arguing for gentiles not being under the law seek to provide exegetical evidence for their position. Moreover, it is true, though, that they approach the related texts with a theological presupposition that the gentiles never possessed the law.

Thus, in this study, two tasks will be carried out to prove the thesis: (1) I will provide exegetical evidence for seeing that gentiles are under the law in Paul and (2) I will explore the possible theological background for Paul's placing lawless gentiles under the law.

In this book, however, the second task will be dealt with first as a theoretical foundation for the later exegetical work pertaining to Pauline texts. Literature of Second Temple Judaism and the Greco-Roman world shall be scrutinized to uncover the possible background of Paul's concept of law and its relationship to the gentiles. The book then will engage in exegetical studies on key texts of Paul relative to the law and gentiles by way of historical-grammatical research. It shall seek to answer the question concerning whether he indicates that gentiles, despite not having the law, are under the law. Among Paul's letters, Romans and Galatians will be specifically examined to provide exegetical evidence for Paul's placing gentiles under the law, because these two letters deal with the law more frequently than any other of his letters do. When a text is explored, its context will be carefully examined to determine its own meaning in the individual letter of Paul.

A SURVEY OF VIEWS ON PAUL'S UNDERSTANDING OF THE LAW AND GENTILES

I will survey scholars' interpretation of some key Pauline texts as to their understanding of Paul in his view of the law and gentiles. In this part, some of the highly debated passages in Galatians and Romans, more specifically Gal 3:13 and Rom 2:14–16, will be used as an example to present scholars'

---

5. Paul's gospel was not preached in vacuum. His gospel was preached effectively in the interaction with his contemporary context. Huttunen rightly says that "we cannot think *a priori* that Paul's treatment of law is somehow immune to the Greco-Roman context in which he worked. On the contrary, the assumption should be that Paul's sayings on law—like any other thing he said—were uttered under the influence of the Greco-Roman context." Huttunen, *Paul and Epictetus on Law*, 2.

controversial understanding of Paul regarding the relationship between the law and gentiles. Scholars' views on other passages of Galatians and Romans will be introduced and evaluated in the following chapters when I examine Galatians and Romans in detail to prove this book's thesis.

Galatians 3:13

Numerous significant New Testament scholars have espoused the concept that gentiles are excluded in the third-person plural in Gal 3:13 (so-called "exclusive" meaning), saying that gentiles are not under the law. Conversely, many other scholars have been voicing the idea that Paul includes gentiles in "we/us" (so-called "inclusive" meaning), concluding that both Jews and gentiles are under the curse of the law, from which Christ had to redeem them.

The proponents of the exclusive meaning are Hans Dieter Betz, Richard Hays, N. T. Wright, Terence L. Donaldson, and B. Witherington,[6] among others.[7] The supporters of the inclusive meaning are F. F. Bruce, Heikki Räisänen, Brice L. Martin, Richard N. Longenecker, and Timothy George,[8] among others.[9]

H. D. Betz contends that ἡμᾶς in Gal 3:13 and τοὺς ὑπὸ νόμον in Gal 4:5 refer to Jewish Christians.[10] The reasons provided for his case are that (1) Gal 3:10, 13, 22–24, and 4:3–5 refer back to 2:15, where Paul says "we are Jews by nature (ἡμεῖς φύσει Ἰουδαῖοι) and not sinners from among the gentiles." (2) According to the context, "we" means Jewish Christians. (3) Gentiles were not under the curse of the law because they were not "under the Torah," but "under the 'elements of the world.'" (4) "The universal reign

6. Betz, *Galatians*, 148; Hays, *Faith of Jesus Christ*, 78, 102–11; Wright, *Climax of the Covenant*, 143, 151–52; Donaldson, "'Curse of the Law' and the Inclusion of the Gentiles," 95–98; Witherington, *Grace in Galatia*, 236.

7. Other scholars supporting this perspective include Burton, *Epistle to the Galatians*, 169; Robinson, "Distinction between Jewish and Gentile Believers in Galatians," 34–35; Braswell, "Blessing of Abraham versus 'the Curse of the Law,'" 74, 79; Matera, *Galatians*, 120, 124; Hong, "Being 'Under the Law' in Galatians," 362.

8. Bruce, *Epistle to the Galatians*, 166–67; Räisänen, *Paul and the Law*, 19–20; Martin, *Christ and the Law in Paul*, 101–04; Longenecker, *Galatians*, 121; George, *Galatians*, 237.

9. Other scholars arguing for the inclusive meaning of "we" include Oepke, *Der Brief des Paulus an die Galater*, 107; Rohde, *Der Brief des Paulus an die Galater*, 145; Hansen, *Abraham in Galatians*, 123; Martyn, *Galatians*, 317–18; Young, "Who's Cursed—and Why? (Galatians 3:10–14)," 90; Wisdom, *Blessing for the Nations and the Curse of the Law*, 191; Tolmie, *Persuading the Galatians*, 121; Schreiner, *Galatians*, 215; de Boer, *Galatians*, 209; Moo, *Galatians*, 213; Harmon, *Galatians*, 159.

10. Betz, *Galatians*, 148, 208.

of law and sin over both the Jew and the Gentile is staged clearly only in Romans, not in Galatians."[11]

According to Richard Hays, Paul refers to Jews by "us" in Gal 3:13 due to the fact that "ἡμᾶς is immediately set in juxtaposition to τὰ ἔθνη."[12] Hays understands *us* (ἡμᾶς) in verse 13 to mean the Jews, while he insists that the third-person plural implied in "λάβωμεν" in verse 14 "includes Jews and Gentiles together."[13] As a result, he explains verses 13–14 in this way: "Christ's redemptive work removed the curse from *Israel* so that the blessing of Abraham (v. 8) can come to Gentiles and so that 'we' (= all God's people, Jews and Gentiles together) can receive the promise of the Spirit."[14] His exclusive understanding of "ἡμᾶς" in verse 13 is based on his presupposition that "those who are of the works of the Law (Ὅσοι γὰρ ἐξ ἔργων νόμου εἰσίν)," in verse 10, means "those whose identity is derived from works of Law."[15] According to Hays, because the Jews identify themselves by works of law and, thereby, are under the curse of the law, gentiles cannot be said to be under the curse of the law. In addition, Hays recognizes that the curses of the law are applicable to Israel as a whole. The whole people of Israel were sent away into exile because of their disobedience.[16]

Terence L. Donaldson believes—regarding Gal 3:13—that *Israel* was redeemed from the law's curse by the cross of Christ, so that *gentiles* might receive Abraham's blessing. Therefore, he considers that there are two steps between "cross" and "gentiles":[17] first is Israel's redemption from the curse of the law and second is Abraham's blessing reaching the gentiles. According to Donaldson, Paul expresses Israel's plight as being "under the curse of the law" (3:13), "confined under the law (pedagogue)" (3:25), and "under the law and the elemental spirits" (4:3, 5). Christ's identification with Israel's plight is described as "becoming a curse for us" (3:13) and "born under the law" (4:4).

The position N. T. Wright holds regarding "we" and "us" in Gal 3:13–14 is that both of them mean Jewish Christians (exclusive meaning). The apparent reason he provides for his case is that "it is Jews who are under Torah."[18]

---

11. Betz, *Galatians*, 148.

12. Hays, *Faith of Jesus Christ*, 79n18.

13. Hays, *Faith of Jesus Christ*, 104; Hays, *Letter to the Galatians*, 262.

14. Hays, *Letter to the Galatians*, 257.

15. Hays, *Letter to the Galatians*, 257. In line with Martyn, Hays understands οἱ ἐκ πίστεως in v. 7 as "those whose identity is derived from faith." See Hays, *Letter to the Galatians*, 255, 257; Martyn, *Galatians*, 299.

16. Hays, *Letter to the Galatians*, 258–59.

17. Donaldson, "'Curse of the Law' and the Inclusion of the Gentiles," 97.

18. Wright, *Climax of the Covenant*, 143.

Furthermore, Wright insists that Paul does not indicate gentiles were under the Torah in Gal 4:1–11. Nor are gentiles under the στοιχεῖα. According to N. T. Wright's knowledge of Paul, it is absurd to think that Paul understands gentiles to be under the Mosaic law "they never possessed."[19] Colossians 2:14–23 is the only place where he finds that Paul seemingly places gentiles under the Torah "by a peculiar sort of extension." Wright doubts, however, whether Colossians could be a solid ground for the exegesis of Galatians. For Wright, the curse of the law is Israel's exile and subjugation to a foreign power due to the nation's disobedience. In this theological paradigm, there is no room for gentiles to be included as people under the curse.

On the other hand, Brice L. Martin feels that gentiles are also under the law and its curse [20] He insists, citing Rom 2:14–16, that gentiles know the law sufficiently enough to be enslaved and condemned, although they do not have the law given to Israel on Sinai. Concerning Galatians, Martin understands "we" in Gal 3:13, 23, 25 to be both Jews and gentiles, concluding "'we' (Gal 3:13, 25) and the universal context of the work of Christ (Gal 3:13; 4:5) indicate that even the gentile is *hypo nomon* and therefore under the curse of the law."[21]

Timothy George believes that Jews and gentiles are under the law in Paul as well. He writes:

> As Paul argued in Rom 1–3, both Jews and Gentiles are 'under the law,' albeit in very different ways. . . . Thus the "us" of 3:13— those whom Christ has redeemed from the curse of the law— are not merely Jewish Christians but instead all the children of God, Jews and Gentiles.[22]

In his comment on Gal 4:4, Timothy George understands Jesus' birth "under the law" as referring to Christ being a Jewish man.[23] Nevertheless, when he interprets the purpose of Jesus being "born under the law" in 4:5, i.e., to redeem *those who were under the law*, George maintains seemingly inconsistently that Christ's redemptive work is related not only to the Jews but also to the gentiles, because Jews and gentiles alike are under the law.[24]

---

19. Wright, *Climax of the Covenant*, 143.

20. Martin, *Christ and the Law in Paul*, 100–104.

21. Martin, *Christ and the Law in Paul*, 104. Italics original.

22. George, *Galatians*, 233.

23. George, *Galatians*, 303.

24. George, *Galatians*, 304.

Romans 2:14–16

Romans 2:14–16 is another place where Paul's understanding of the relationship between the law and gentiles can be found. Along with Brice L. Martin and Timothy George, who both contend that gentiles are under the law in Rom 2:14–16, other scholars also argue that Paul places gentiles under the law in that same biblical passage.

Richard H. Bell states that "Paul is establishing in vv. 14–16 that Gentiles also have a law by which they will be judged and this judgment will be through Jesus Christ."[25] He claims that Paul would have thought of the law's cosmic dimension.[26] He also argues that Rom 7:7–13 refers to Adam and the law, which allegedly existed in Adam's time.[27]

Mark A. Seifrid understands Rom 2:14–15 in light of Rom 1:18–32, in which he detects natural revelation.[28] The created order reveals not only a knowledge of God, the creator, but a knowledge of his will. Consequently, gentiles do the things of the law by nature (2:14). He finds the knowledge of God's will written in gentiles' hearts, by creational revelation, to be "equal to the manifestation of his will in the law of Moses."[29]

As the main point of Rom 2:14–15, Thomas R. Schreiner states that "Gentiles possess the law," too.[30] Although Schreiner acknowledges that gentiles do not have the Mosaic law, he understands Paul to be saying that they possess the law in terms of the Mosaic law's moral norms.[31] According to Schreiner, the "work of the law" written in the hearts of gentiles "refers to the commands contained in the Mosaic law," and gentiles occasionally obey the law's commands.[32] Supporting Bornkamm, Wilckens, and Stott, Schreiner conjectures that Paul employs a natural-law concept of Greek when he writes "the work of the law written in their hearts," a "law to themselves (ἑαυτοῖς εἰσιν νόμος)" and "conscience (συνείδησις)."[33]

Some scholars, though, evade the issue that Paul regards gentiles to be under the law in Rom 2:14–15 by arguing that the gentiles in these verses are gentile *Christians.* Simon J. Gathercole upholding this position enumerates

25. Bell, *No One Seeks for God,* 152.

26. Bell, *No One Seeks for God,* 157.

27. Bell, *No One Seeks for God,* See especially n122.

28. Seifrid, *Christ, Our Righteousness,* 48–54.

29. Seifrid, *Christ, Our Righteousness,* 54.

30. Schreiner, *Romans,* 121.

31. Schreiner, *Romans,* 121.

32. Schreiner, *Romans,* 122.

33. Schreiner, *Romans,* 122–24; Bornkamm, *Studien zu Antike und Urchristentum,* 101–102; Wilckens, *Der Brief an die Römer,* 134; Stott, *Romans,* 87.

those who support this line of interpretation: Ambrosiaster, Augustine of Hippo, W. Mundle, Karl Barth, F. Flückiger, J. B. Souček, C. E. B. Cranfield, R. Bergmeier, and N. T. Wright.[34]

Gathercole contends that φύσει in verse 14 modifies what precedes it, making the sense that "those without Torah *by birthright*" rather than that "doing *by nature* the things of the law." Based on the parallels between Rom 2:25–29 and 2:13–16, Gathercole—who observes 2:25–29 as referring to Christian gentiles—conjectures that the 2:14–16 passage has Christian gentiles in mind. For Gathercole, Jer 31:33 (38:33 LXX) presents more evidence for reading the "work of the law written in their hearts," in Rom 2:15, as the internalization of the Torah for Christian gentiles living in the new-covenant era. In Gathercole's contention against rendering φύσει as "doing *by nature* the things of the law," he reveals his negative view about gentiles carrying out the law, saying "it would be unparalleled in Paul's thought to say that Gentiles had the spontaneous, natural ability to carry out even *elements* of Torah" (emphasis original).[35]

The fact that Paul places gentiles not having the law under the law appears to cause some to be perplexed, such as Heikki Räisänen. He sees that Paul puts gentiles under the curse of the law in Gal 3:13–14, with his reference to them by the first-person plural.[36] Moreover, he observes that Paul distinguishes Jews from gentiles in terms of their possession of the law, i.e., Jews under the law and gentiles without the law. From these observations, Räisänen draws the conclusion that these are the "pointers to Paul's *personal theological problems*" because of his [Paul's] confusion (italics original).[37] He holds that "contradictions and tensions have to be *accepted* as *constant* features of Paul's theology of the law. They are not simply of an accidental or peripheral nature" (italics original).[38]

As we have seen above briefly, not all find that Paul places lawless gentiles under the law.[39] This is due partly to the result of their exegetical work, and/or partly to their theological presupposition that Paul cannot say gentiles are under the law, because he mentions gentiles as being without the law. As a result, this book's second chapter shall seek to prove that Paul's

---

34. Gathercole, "Law unto Themselves," 28–30. See this article for the following explanation.

35. Gathercole, "Law unto Themselves," 37.

36. Räisänen, *Paul and the Law*, 18–23.

37. Räisänen, *Paul and the Law*, 12.

38. Räisänen, *Paul and the Law*, 11. See also Westerholm's summary of Räisänen's view. Westerholm, *Perspectives Old and New on Paul*, 171–77.

39. Brian Rosner also insists that gentiles are not under the law. See Rosner, *Paul and the Law*, 51–56.

placing lawless gentiles under the law is not unthinkable in Hellenistic Judaism's milieu. The second chapter is, thus, expected to provide a possible theological background for Paul placing gentiles under the law that they never possessed. Having established a theoretical foundation, the next focus will be on Romans (Chap. 3) and Galatians (Chap. 4) to demonstrate exegetically that Paul places gentiles under the law and its curse, from which Christ died to redeem them as well as Jews. Finally, the entire discussion shall be summarized and concluded in the fifth chapter.

CHAPTER 2

The Background of Paul's Understanding of the Law and Gentiles in Hellenistic Judaism and Greco-Roman World

INTRODUCTION

THE IDEA THAT PAUL places lawless gentiles under the law and its curse is not entirely unthinkable because a similar notion can be found in the literature of Hellenistic Judaism. In this chapter, Hellenistic Judaism's notion of gentiles being under the law shall be examined. This chapter's purpose is not to suggest that Hellenism or Judaism is the origin of Paul's placing gentiles under the law but to demonstrate that his placing gentiles under the law has common ground in Hellenistic Judaism. Thus, this chapter is expected to provide a theoretical foundation for interpreting Paul's letters with the view that he places gentiles under the law, especially in his discussion about gentiles' condemnation and salvation.

MOSAIC LAW AND NATURAL LAW IN HELLENISTIC JUDAISM

It is apparent that the Mosaic law was given to Israel on Mount Sinai. Do gentiles then have nothing to do with it? When the literature of Hellenistic Judaism is considered, it can be observed that gentiles are placed under the

Mosaic law as well. The Mosaic law's universal validity is explained in Hellenistic Judaism through the close correlation between the Mosaic law and the natural law. Before investigating this phenomenon, it would be useful to comprehend the Greek thought of the law because the Jewish idea of the law must have encountered the Greek thought of the law during the Hellenistic period.[1]

The Law in Greek Thought

The Greek conception of the law is well-explained by John W. Martens in his book *One God, One Law*.[2] Although Greek thinkers generally consider the written law to be good, they believe that there is a "higher" law, which is described as nature's law, the unwritten law, and the living law. Such a concept of laws is based on "a belief in the divine ordering of the world."[3] The world's divine order extends to human law. The law of nature, which is unwritten law, is "valid for everyone everywhere," unlike the written law.[4] As a result, this law transcends human boundaries. Socrates terms unwritten law as law which comes from God.[5] Furthermore, Demosthenes and Thucydides also consider unwritten law as a borderless, inherent, natural and eternal law.[6]

Udo Schnelle likewise comments on the law in Greco-Roman thought, "In the first century there was also a widespread awareness that in addition to the countless individual laws, there is *one* law."[7] This one law is the true and valid law, which already existed before the coming of particular written laws. This law is recognized as the "law of nature."

Universal Law in Hellenistic Judaism

The Mosaic law's universality is expressed in various ways in Hellenistic Judaism. One of the characteristics in Hellenistic Judaism's presenting the Mosaic law's universal validity is its identifying wisdom with the Mosaic

1. The encounter between Hellenism and Judaism is believed to have started in the fourth century BC. Hengel, *Judaism and Hellenism*, 1–3.

2. Martens, *One God, One Law*.

3. Martens, *One God, One Law*, 1.

4. Martens, *One God, One Law*, 7.

5. Martens, *One God, One Law*, 8.

6. Martens, *One God, One Law*, 8–9.

7. Schnelle, *Apostle Paul*, 507.

law. In Sirach, wisdom is described just like the natural law in Hellenism and then is identified with the Mosaic law (Sir 1:1–10, 24:1–23). Identifying wisdom with the Mosaic law is thus similar to Hellenism's connecting the natural law to the written laws. Numerous scholars have observed this similarity. Markus Bockmuehl points out that Ben Sira's expression of wisdom's cosmic universality in nature is in agreement with contemporary Hellenistic thought.[8] J. Marböck insists that "it was the Stoic popular philosophy which caused Ben Sira to combine the Torah and cosmic wisdom."[9]

Some scholars such as Joseph Blenkinsopp argue that there is a similarity between the wisdom in Sirach and the Hellenistic deity myth. Blenkinsopp, commenting on Sir 24:1–12, assumes that the wisdom of Ben Sira is modeled on the Egyptian goddess Isis (Maat) or a Syro-Palestinian counterpart like Astarte.[10] He explains the epiphany of Isis as described in book XI of the *Metamorphoses* of Apuleius of Madaura: "Isis declares her praises and titles in the first person, describes how she presided over Creation . . . and how she came down from her heavenly abode to search throughout the world for a place in which to establish her cult." Blenkinsopp concludes that Ben Sira implemented an indigenized form of the Isis aretalogy to claim for the Torah a universal significance.[11] In addition, Martin Hengel argues that wisdom's cosmic universality in Sir 24 and the hymn to wisdom in Sir 1:1–20 are echoes of the Isis aretalogy.[12] He further finds an analogy from the Stoic Logos regarding Sirach's wisdom: "The 'universal law' identical with the Logos which ordered the world harmoniously, at the same time formed the moral norm for human conduct."[13] Similarly, John Collins notes that "There are clear similarities between the Jewish concept of wisdom and

---

8. Bockmuehl, *Jewish Law in Gentile Churches*, 98. John Collins provides some other examples of the Hellenistic idea of universal law in nature: "Zeno, the founder of Stoicism, wrote that 'the universal law [*nomos*], which is true reason [*logos*] permeating everything, is identical with Zeus, the guide of the arrangement of all things' (Diogenes Laertius 7.88; cf. Cicero, *De re publica* 3.33; *De legibus* 1.16, 18:2.8)." "In Cicero's formulation, 'Law is the highest reason, implanted in nature, which commands what ought to be done, and forbids the opposite'(n. Cicero, *De legibus* 1.18)." Collins, *Jewish Wisdom in the Hellenistic Age*, 60.

9. Cited from Eckhard Schnabel, who refers to Marböck. Schanbel, *Law and Wisdom from Ben Sira to Paul*, 84; and Marböck, "Gesetz und Weisheit: Zum Verständnis des Gesetzes bei Jesus Sirach," 20.

10. Blenkinsopp, *Wisdom and Law in the Old Testament*, 165.

11. Blenkinsopp, *Wisdom and Law in the Old Testament*, 166.

12. Hengel states, "Sir 24.5f. also points in a more mythological form—presumably taken over from the Isis aretalogy—to this cosmic universality of wisdom." See Hengel, *Judaism and Hellenism*, 158–59.

13. Hengel, *Judaism and Hellenism*, 160.

the Stoic Logos, between the Jewish notion of a law given at creation and the Stoic law of nature."[14]

Judaism and Hellenism in Terms of Natural Law

Is the descending of wisdom on Israel in Sir 24 really Ben Sira's contextualization of the Isis aretalogy for his own purpose? Is Ben Sira's idea of the cosmic universality of wisdom (identified with the law) in nature the result of Hellenism, in which the law of nature or the unwritten law is universal and extends to human law? Is the idea of universal wisdom in Sirach influenced by Stoic 'Logos'? Bockmuehl seems to argue for Ben Sira's indebtedness to Hellenism for his idea of natural law, when affirming that "it is clear from Sir 42:15—43:33 and elsewhere that Ben Sira does have a kind of natural theology; like the book of Wisdom, indeed, he follows contemporary Hellenistic thought in stressing the cosmic universality of wisdom in nature."[15]

Ben Sira's idea of wisdom's cosmic universality in creation demonstrates the idea of natural law, especially because Ben Sira equates the wisdom in creation with the law of Moses.[16] According to the cosmic law of nature, all human beings are obligated to decide between life and death, good and evil. Considering the Hellenistic understanding of law, it is clear that there are similarities between Ben Sira's idea of the cosmic universality of law (wisdom) in creation and the Hellenistic view of natural law. As in the Hellenistic view, natural law is valid for everyone everywhere; wisdom in Sirach is also universal (Sir 1:9–10; 24:3–6). In the Hellenistic view, the "law of nature" existed as true law before the written law comes into being. Likewise, lady wisdom in Sirach praises herself that "over every people and nation I have held sway" (Sir 24:6) before making her dwelling in Israel as the Mosaic law (Sir 24:8–12).

14. Collins, *Jewish Wisdom in the Hellenistic Age*, 60.

15. Bockmuehl, *Jewish Law in Gentile Churches*, 98.

16. Helmut Koester claims that "most probably" Philo was the creator of the natural-law theory. However, it is not convincing, because the natural-law theory can be already found in Sirach. Koester, "ΝΟΜΟΣ ΦΥΣΕΩΣ: The Concept of Natural Law in Greek Thought," in *Religions in Antiquity*, 540. David T. Runia also points out that Koester fails to consider Cicero for the law of nature. Philo, *On the Creation of the Cosmos according to Moses*, 107. Concluding his discussion on natural law in Second Temple Judaism, Bockmuehl confirms that "Philo's development of natural law theory is in fact indebted not only to Stoic ideas of the preceding two generations, but to a well-documented and long-standing tradition within Second Temple Judaism itself." Bockmuehl, *Jewish Law in Gentile Churches*, 111.

All similar expressions and ideas found in Sirach (and other Jewish sources) in agreement with Greek literature and philosophy, however, may not simply be attributed to Hellenism. It cannot be stated that the idea of natural law in Sirach originated exclusively from Judaism or Hellenism. As David Novak points out, natural law is "natural," in other words, "inherently *universal*."[17] Hence, it cannot be maintained that natural law is a concept constructed within Judaism or Hellenism alone. Inasmuch as Hellenism possesses its own way of thinking about the natural law, so Judaism has its own way of thinking, for instance, the concept of Noahide law later in rabbinic Judaism.[18]

Regarding the Wisdom of Solomon, John J. Collins conjectures that the idea that "human beings could arrive at the knowledge of God without the aid of special revelation" becomes possible by Greek philosophical presuppositions of the Wisdom of Solomon's author.[19] When the Second Temple Jewish literature, including the Wisdom of Solomon and Sirach, is observed, though, the Jewish concept of creation by the one true God, and Jewish faith in God the creator seem to play important roles in thinking that God and his will can be known by nature, which he formed. Hellenistic Jewish authors' concept of the natural law seems not to have originated exclusively from Greek philosophical presuppositions.

The ideas of natural law and natural theology exist in the Old Testament and other Jewish traditions. Chapters 1–11 in Genesis illustrate the fact that everything proceeds according to God's command.[20] James Barr refers to Pss 19, 104, and 119 as examples in his discussion regarding natural theology.[21] Pertaining to Ps 119:89–92, Jon D. Levenson mentions:

> In other words, the commandments that the psalmist practices, even those which may be Pentateuchal, constitute a kind of revealed natural law. They enable him to bring his own life into harmony with the rhythm of the cosmos and to have access to the creative and life-giving energy that drives the world.[22]

17. Novak, *Natural Law in Judaism*, 191.

18. Novak insists that "we should say that with the concept of Noahide law, Jewish thinkers have an authentically Jewish way to engage in thinking natural law. And they can offer their thinking both within and without their own community, although the latter requires the additional intellectual work of translation." Novak, *Natural Law in Judaism*, 191.

19. Collins, "Natural Theology and Biblical Tradition," 4–5.

20. Bockmuehl, *Jewish Law in Gentile Churches*, 89. He continues to say that there is never any "lawless moment" in the first through the eleventh chapters of Genesis.

21. Barr, *Biblical Faith and Natural Theology*, 81–90.

22. Levenson, "The Sources of Torah" in *Ancient Israelite Religion*, 569. It is cited as

Bockmuehl provides some additional texts which reflect natural law, such as Gen 6:5, 11–13, 20:3–4, 34:7; Pss 29, 33, 147; Isa 1:2–3; Amos 1:9, 6:12; Job 31:13–15; Tob 4:15; Wis 14:22–29; 4 Macc 1:1–6, 18; and *Letter of Aristeas* 143 ("set down everything similarly in regard to natural reasoning").[23] Bockmuehl attests that the *Testament of Naphtali* shows a moral analogy from creation:

> Sun, moon and stars do not alter their order; thus you should not alter the Law of God by the disorder of your actions. The gentiles, because they wandered astray and forsook the Lord, have changed the order, and have devoted themselves to stones and sticks, patterning themselves after wandering spirits. But you, my children, shall not be like that: in the firmament, in the earth, and in the sea, in all the products of his workmanship discern the Lord who made all things, so that you do not become like Sodom, which departed from the order of nature. Likewise the Watchers departed from nature's order; the Lord pronounced a curse on them at the Flood. On their account he ordered that the earth be without dweller or produce.[24]

Pseudo-Phocylides provides a similar example:

> Do not envy (your) friends their goods, do not fix reproach (upon them). The heavenly ones also are without envy toward each other. The moon does not envy the much stronger beams of the sun, nor the earth the heavenly heights though it is below, nor the rivers the seas. They are always in concord. For if there were strife among the blessed ones, heaven would not stand firm.[25]

The idea of the natural law can be identified in many places in the works of Philo and of Josephus.[26] Philo's natural law concept is found in *De Vita Mosis*, in which he discusses why Moses started his law book with the history about the creation of the universe rather than about people's deeds:

> He [Moses] wished to shew two most essential things: first that the Father and Maker of the world was in the truest sense also its Lawgiver, secondly that he who would observe the laws will

---

well by Barr, *Biblical Faith and Natural Theology*, 90.

23. For details, see Bockmuehl, *Jewish Law in Gentile Churches*, 87–101.

24. *Test. Naph.* 3:2–5; and Bockmuehl, *Jewish Law in Gentile Churches*, 101.

25. *Ps.-Phoc.*, 70–75, from Van Der Horst, "Pseudo-Phocylides," 576. It is also cited by Bockmuehl, *Jewish Law in Gentile Churches*, 102.

26. See Bockmuehl, *Jewish Law in Gentile Churches*, 107–10.

accept gladly the duty of following nature and live in accordance with the ordering of the universe, so that his deeds are attuned to harmony with his words and his words with his deeds.[27]

In *Jewish Antiquities*, Josephus employs the law of nature as a synonym with the will of God.[28] After recording the people's grief about Moses' upcoming death, Josephus describes Moses' state of mind as follows:

> For although he was always persuaded that he ought not to be cast down at the approach of death, since the undergoing it was agreeable to the will of God and the law of nature, yet what the people did so overbore him that he wept himself.[29]

From this observation of the natural law concept in the Old Testament and Jewish tradition, it can be proven that the idea of the natural law found in Hellenistic Judaism did not solely originate in Hellenism or Judaism. The idea of the natural law in Hellenistic Judaism is a natural ramification of the Jewish understanding of God as creator and judge of the universe. Hellenistic Jews were most likely to have expressed their recognition of the law and God with more focus on the idea of the natural law in a Hellenistic context, with similar expressions found in Greco-Roman literature for various reasons.

For Ben Sira, Hellenism seems to have been "the decisive motive force" for identifying wisdom with the Mosaic law.[30] According to Martin Hengel, the integration of law and wisdom had already existed in Jewish wisdom speculation as found in Deut 4:16, "where God's commandments are called the wisdom of Israel over against the nations."[31] This integration was further developed, though, in Hellenism's context. Schnabel provides a similar argument. He thinks that the correlation of wisdom and the law has an Old Testament background. He refers to Deut 4:6–8, "Jer 8,8; Mal 2, 6–7 (?); Ezr 7,6.10.25, and the so-called wisdom-psalms Ps 1; 19; 119."[32] Identification of wisdom and law in Sirach, according to Schnabel, was "facilitated, if not prompted, by the historical circumstances."[33] Hengel believes that Ben Sira

---

27. *Mos.* 2.48. *Philo with an English Translation by F. H. Colson*, vol. 6, LCL 289, 473.

28. Bockmuehl refers to *Ant.* 4.8.48 §322 and 17.5.3 §95 as examples. In addition, he points to *Ag. Ap.* 2.22–30 §190–219 as the place, in which the Torah can be understood according to the law of nature. Bockmuehl, *Jewish Law in Gentile Churches*, 109–10.

29. *Ant.* 4.8.48 §322. Josephus, *New Complete Works of Josephus*, 164.

30. Hengel, *Judaism and Hellenism*, 162.

31. Hengel, *Judaism and Hellenism*, 161

32. Schnabel, *Law and Wisdom from Ben Sira to Paul*, 84.

33. Schnabel, *Law and Wisdom from Ben Sira to Paul*, 87.

might have found a number of Stoic conceptions to be "helpful in his apologetic and polemic statement" and adopted them to his "Jewish belief."[34]

Natural Law and Common Ethics

The idea of natural law was functioning in Hellenistic Judaism to solve the tension between Judaism and Hellenism in terms of morality. Natural law can be the ground from which Mosaic law claims itself as a norm for the ethics of the Hellenized world due to the fact that the written law of Moses is a copy or the embodiment of nature's unwritten law.

Sirach believes that God showed human beings "good and evil" and put "the fear of him" into their hearts in creation (Sir 17:7b, 8a). This means that even foreign lands have moral standards. Thus, good and evil can be found in foreign lands among those who live under the law of nature. The sage can learn or test (ἐπείρασεν [Sir 39:4 BGT]) good and evil in foreign lands because moral standards given to humans in creation can be valid there as well. As Menahem Kister aptly comments, Ben Sira, in Sir 39:4, claims that "the sage has to be exposed to the moral standards of foreign countries."[35] For Ben Sira, the "good" is "to live according to wisdom" (Sir 51:18). In foreign lands, the "good" can be observed among those who live according to the natural law, which is given to them by God, the creator. Concerning the role of natural law in Judaism, David Novak mentions in the conclusion of his book, *Natural Law in Judaism*, "Natural law is that which makes Jewish moral discourse possible in an intercultural world."[36] In this respect, Paul might have also utilized the concept of natural law in indicting gentiles for moral failure before God, although he presents Mosaic law as a written standard to prove such.

The Qumran community shows the ethics based on the order of creation in Sap. Work A (4Q415/416/417/418/423/1Q26) and 4Q422 (4Qpara-GenExod) employing Genesis chapters 1–3 and 8–9, and Ps 8.[37] These texts regard people's place in God's creation and their role in the world created by the Lord "in the different fields of human experience: family, agriculture, wealth, property, finances, relation to God and fellow men, *etc.*"[38]

---

34. Hengel, *Judaism and Hellenism*, 148.

35. Kister, "Wisdom Literature and Its Relation to Other Genres: From Ben Sira to Mysteries," 14.

36. Novak, *Natural Law in Judaism*, 178.

37. Elgvin, "Admonition Texts from Qumran Cave 4," 186–89.

38. Elgvin, "Admonition Texts from Qumran Cave 4," 188.

Gregory E. Sterling delves into whether there was a common ethic in Second Temple Judaism.[39] After reading through Qumran and Philo of Alexandria, Josephus and Pseudo-Phocylides, Sterling observes that "there was a common group of *topoi* that formed the basis for ethical instruction in the Diaspora."[40] According to him, Leviticus chapters 19–20 and 22 and Deuteronomy chapter 22 were most often implemented for ethical instruction in the diaspora and, in some cases, ethical instruction from the larger world was gathered. The authors of the Second Temple Judaism period incorporated moral traditions from the larger Greco-Roman world into their moral codes.[41] He recognizes the use of Greek virtues to describe Torah instruction to be the Alexandrian attempt to present Judaism as a form of Hellenistic philosophy.[42] The Jews' moral discourse with gentiles in the Hellenized world seems to have been made possible by emphasizing the Mosaic law's universalistic aspect in relationship with the natural law.

Natural Law and Mosaic Law

The tension between the universalistic understanding of the law and the particularistic attachment of it to Israel is observed in Sirach because the wisdom in creation (universal) is related to the Torah (particular) in Sir 24.[43] Natural law—wisdom—can be applied to all creation because wisdom was created prior to all other things (Sir 1:4), and God poured her out to all his works (Sir 1:9). Although Ben Sira emphasizes the Mosaic law as embodied wisdom to Israel, he does not totally preclude gentiles' access to wisdom, which is implanted in nature.

The Mosaic law and natural law possess similarities and differences. The Mosaic law was given to Israel (Sir 24:7–11), whereas natural law is provided to all. The Mosaic law is written law, whereas natural law is unwritten law. Sirach shows that the natural law and Mosaic law have the same origin, namely—God the creator—who created wisdom. Both of them reveal God's will in varying degrees.

In Sirach, the natural law and Mosaic law are closely related to each other by the link of wisdom. Therefore, one may think that the natural law

39. Sterling, "Was There a Common Ethic in Second Temple Judaism?," 171–94.

40. Sterling, "Was There a Common Ethic in Second Temple Judaism?," 193.

41. Sterling, "Was There a Common Ethic in Second Temple Judaism?," 184.

42. Sterling, "Was There a Common Ethic in Second Temple Judaism?," 171.

43. Collins notes that the tension between the universalistic and particularistic aspect of the law is quite typical of Diaspora Judaism in the Hellenistic period. Collins, *Between Athens and Jerusalem*, 165.

appears to be the prototype of the Mosaic law, and it was actualized as the law of Israel at a certain point of salvation history. Others may find the pre-existence of the Mosaic law in creation, when wisdom covers all the earth.[44] When Ben Sira declares that Abraham observed the law of the most high (νόμον ὑψίστου, Sir 44:20), he might have said this in light of his understanding of wisdom, which existed as a prototype of the Mosaic law even before the Mosaic Law was formed. Interestingly, Dianne Bergant regards the establishment of cosmic wisdom in the midst of Israel (Sir 24:8–10) as having been decided in the primordial realm, and she views this fact as part of the very structure of the created cosmos.[45]

Jewish writers could present Judaism as a universal religion by observing that it agrees with the laws of nature.[46] Relying on the concept of natural law, Hellenistic Judaism tends to apply Mosaic law not only to Jews but to gentiles as well. In the section of "Eulogy of the Jews" in the Third Sibyl, the law is applied to other nations as well as to the Jews:

> They are mindful of holy wedlock, and they do not engage in impious intercourse with male children, as do Phoenicians, Egyptians, and Romans, spacious Greece and many nations of others, Persians and Galatians and all Asia, transgressing the holy law of immortal God, which they transgressed.[47]

Collins interprets the Third Sybil in terms of the natural law, explaining that "the other nations, too, can be condemned for failing to keep the law (3:599–600). The sybil, like Romans 1 and Wisdom of Solomon 13, seems to presume that the essential law is known to everyone by nature. In fact, the requirement of the sibyl could be seen to a great extent in terms of natural law."[48]

Gentiles under the Law in Hellenistic Judaism and the Greco-Roman World

Although the Mosaic law is recognized as a special gift to Israel, its universal validity is expressed in Hellenistic Judaism and the Greco-Roman world. Particularly in the context of God's judgment of gentiles, the Mosaic law is

44. The Torah's preexistence is later affirmed in rabbinic writings, e.g., *Sifre Deut.* 37; *b. Pesah* 54 a; *b. Ned.* 39b; and *Bereshith Rabba* 1.1.

45. Bergant, *Israel's Wisdom Literature*, 173.

46. Collins, *Between Athens and Jerusalem*, 160.

47. Third Sybil 595–600, from Collins, "Sibylline Oracles," 375.

48. Collins, "Sibylline Oracles," 162.

referred to as a standard by which they are silenced and judged. The gentiles' being under the Mosaic law is expressed in various ways. Natural law concept plays an important role, however, in applying the Mosaic law to the gentiles, who do not possess it. Sirach provides an example of how Hellenistic Jews connect the Mosaic law to the world by the idea of the natural law. Sirach will be examined first in a rather detailed manner, and other Jewish literature will be studied next.

GENTILES UNDER THE LAW IN SIRACH

Sirach, also called "The Wisdom of Ben Sira" or "Ecclesiasticus," was originally written in Hebrew by Joshua ben Sira in about 180 BC; his grandson translated it into Greek in about 132 BC.[49] The idea that gentiles are under the law is identified in Sirach as well as in Paul's letters.

The conception of natural law and written law appears in Sirach, demonstrating that gentiles are under the law. The idea of natural law plays an important role in the discourse of Hellenistic Jews with outsiders.[50] The ideas of natural law and revealed (or written) law are well-developed in Sirach.[51] In the following, these ideas will be explored by scrutinizing Sirach's understanding of the relationship between natural law and the Mosaic law with the help of his view of wisdom.

Wisdom as the Law of Moses in Sirach

In order to understand Sirach's placing of gentiles under the law, it is useful to see his perspective of Mosaic law in terms of wisdom at the outset. In Sirach, wisdom is identified with the law of Moses. Martin McNamara recognizes that "Ben Sira himself practically identifies wisdom with the law of Moses."[52] He points to Sir 24:23: "All this is the book of the covenant of the Most High God, the law which Moses commanded us as an inheritance

49. Evans, *Ancient Texts for New Testament Studies*, 15.

50. Markus Bockmuehl points out that "although the terminology 'natural' law is not native to Palestinian Judaism, the issue itself has been recognized as foundational to Hellenistic Jewish discourse with outsiders." Bockmuehl, *Jewish Law in Gentile Churches*, xi.

51. Bockmuehl acknowledges that the idea of natural law can be found in Sirach. He seems to underestimate the natural law motif in Sirach, however, when he states that the natural law motif is not highly developed in Sirach. Bockmuehl, *Jewish Law in Gentile Churches*, 111.

52. McNamara, "Some Targum Themes," 310.

for the congregation of Jacob." Shannon Burkes comprehends that "all this" means the wisdom that the immediately preceding poem mentions.[53]

John Collins also recognizes that wisdom is identified with the law of Moses in Sir 24.[54] For Sirach's identification of wisdom with the law, Eckhard Schnabel refers to Sir 19:20, which reads, "The whole of wisdom is fear of the Lord, and in all wisdom there is the fulfillment of the law."[55]

Although some scholars, such as M. Black, say—according to Schnabel—that "the correlation of Torah with wisdom is certainly significant but complete identification is doubtful except in some probably secondary traditions attributed to Ben Sira," Schnabel disagrees. Against M. Black, Schnabel delineates the fact that (1) it is impossible to attribute all passages, which identify law with wisdom, to secondary traditions; and (2) the complete identification of law and wisdom by Ben Sira is recognized and acknowledged by the vast majority of scholars.[56] It is evident that Sirach equates the law of Moses with wisdom.

Wisdom as the Natural Law in Sirach

Wisdom as it is identified with the law of Moses in Sirach can be traced all the way back to the creation. God created wisdom (Sir 1:4—"Wisdom was created before all other things"[57]) before the ages, in the beginning (Sir 24:9—"Before the ages, in the beginning, he created me, and for all the ages I shall not cease to be"). The Lord poured wisdom out on all his works (Sir 1:9). In Sir 24:3–6, wisdom praises herself as the one exercising dominion over heaven, earth, the sea, every people, and all nations:

> I came forth from the mouth of the Most High, and covered the
> earth like a mist. I dwelt in the highest heavens, and my throne
> was in a pillar of cloud. Alone I compassed the vault of heaven
> and traversed the depths of the abyss. Over waves of the sea,

53. Burkes, "Wisdom and Law," 258.

54. Collins, *Jewish Wisdom in the Hellenistic Age*, 54, 57. See also Bergant, *Israel's Wisdom Literature*, 172–77.

55. Schnabel, *Law and Wisdom from Ben Sira to Paul*, 70. Eckhard Schnabel provides explicit evidence (15:1, 17:11, 19:20, 21:11, 24:23, 34:8, 45:5c and d); implicit evidence (1:26, 2:15–16, 6:36, 15:15, 19:24, 24:22, 24:32–33, 33:2–3, 38:34c and d, 39:8, 44:4c, 51:15c and d, 51:30a and b); and secondary passages (1:5, 19:19, Prol 1–3, Prol 12–14, Prol 29, Prol 35–36) for Sirach's identification of wisdom with the law. For details, see Schnabel, *Law and Wisdom from Ben Sira to Paul*, 69–79.

56. Schnabel, *Law and Wisdom from Ben Sira to Paul*, 89n443.

57. All Apocrypha quotations are from the NRSV.

over all the earth, and over every people and nation I have held
sway.

Wisdom ruled over creation. Wisdom covered the earth like a mist
and was enthroned on a pillar of cloud (24:3–4). In this regard, as Collins
states, "the initial revelation of wisdom is in creation itself."[58] Wisdom is
exalted as natural law in Sirach.

Mosaic Law as an Actualization of Natural Law

Wisdom then sought a resting place, and the creator of wisdom chose Zion
and Jerusalem as the dwelling place of wisdom (Sir 24:7–11). The wisdom
revealed in creation was embodied as the Mosaic law to Israel when the
wisdom was commanded to dwell in Jacob (Sir 24:8). In Sir 24:23, wisdom is
identified with "the book of the covenant," which is the Deuteronomic term
for the law of Moses.[59]

Therefore, it might be said that the wisdom had existed as the natural
law in creation before it became the Mosaic law. Collins contends that "the
law revealed to Moses was implicit in creation from the beginning, and so it
is an actualization (the supreme actualization) of natural law."[60] E. P. Sanders realizes similarly that universal wisdom is represented and articulated
in the Mosaic law.[61] Consequently, he considers that the behavior wisdom
teaches in all nations "is identified as obedience to the commandments of
the Jewish covenant."[62] Collins observes that "the identification of the wisdom implanted in creation with the law of Moses has important implica-
tions for the thinking of later Jewish and Christian tradition on the subject
of natural law."[63] Sirach implies that there was natural law, which revealed
the will of God in the beginning. The actualization of this natural law is the
Mosaic law.

Because Sirach connects the natural law with the Mosaic law in terms
of wisdom, the natural law functions like the Mosaic law where the Mosaic
law does not exist. This phenomenon can be observed in some Sirach verses,
including Sir 15:14–17, 17:1–10, and 38:1–15.

---

58. Collins, *Jewish Wisdom in the Hellenistic Age*, 58.

59. Bergant, *Israel's Wisdom Literature*, 174. Hengel cites Deut 4:6 and Pss 1 and
119 as the older examples of the integration of law and wisdom. Hengel, *Judaism and
Hellenism*, 161.

60. Collins, *Jewish Wisdom in the Hellenistic Age*, 58.

61. Sanders, *Paul and Palestinian Judaism*, 331.

62. Sanders, *Paul and Palestinian Judaism*, 331.

63. Collins, *Jewish Wisdom in the Hellenistic Age*, 61.

Natural Law in Sir 15:14–17

The idea of the natural law can be found in Sir 15:14–17:

> It was he who created (ἐποίησεν) humankind in the beginning (ἐξ ἀρχῆς), and he left them in the power of their own free choice. If you choose (θέλῃς), you can keep the commandments (ἐντολὰς), and to act faithfully is a matter of your choice. He has placed before you fire and water; stretch out your hand for whichever you choose. Before each person are life and death, and whichever one chooses will be given.

In this passage, "commandments" likely refer to the Mosaic law. Sirach seems to urge those who are under the Torah to observe the commandments because verse 17 mentions the choice between life and death found in Deut 30:15 and 19. The overall context of Sirach, in which the law predominantly means the Mosaic law, supports this viewpoint. Moreover, Sir 15:14–17 talks of those who are *not* under the Mosaic law, though, because it relates the free choice not only to Israel, but to all human beings created in the beginning. In verse 14, God created humankind (ἄνθρωπον) in the beginning and left them (αὐτὸν) in the power of their own free choice.[64] Di Lella translates this verse literally in this way: "And he placed them in the hand of their free will [yēser]."[65]

Free choice is related to the creation of humans, even before the Mosaic law was given to Israel. All people were given the power to choose from the beginning, not only those who later received the Mosaic law. If free choice is involved with humankind in creation, keeping God's commandments is a matter for all human beings. For instance, Adam and Eve also experienced free choice between life and death. The choice between life and death in verse 17 alludes to Adam as well as to Deut 30, as can be seen in Gen 2:17: "But of the tree of the knowledge of good and evil you shall not eat, for in the day that you eat of it you shall *die* (תָּמוּת)."

Depending on the choice of humans, there is no difference between the law given to Adam and Eve and that given to Israel in terms of life and death. Mentioning Sir 15:14–17, Collins notes that "the law set before Adam

---

64. For the concept of human beings' free will in Judaism, see Laato, *Paul and Judaism*, 67–75.

65. Skehan and Di Lella, *Wisdom of Ben Sira*, 271. Other translations are as follows: (1) "It was he, from the first, when he created humankind, who made them subject to their own free choice." Skehan, *Wisdom of Ben Sira*, 267. (2) "It was he who created him in the beginning, and he left him in the power of his own inclination." MacKenzie, *Sirach*, 72. (3) "When he made man in the beginning, he left him free to take his own decisions." Snaith, *Ecclesiasticus*, 78.

and Eve was no different from the law given to Moses on Mount Sinai. The
law of creation and the law of Sinai are one and the same."[66]

Sirach 15:14–17 presents human responsibility.[67] Human responsibility originated from creation, rather than from the conferring of the Mosaic
law. As a result, it is apparent that human responsibility concerning choices
is not only confined to the Jews under the Mosaic law; it is a matter for
all human beings under the natural law from the start. All human beings
have responsibility for choices between life and death before the creator.[68]
Although Sirach is generally viewed as referring to the free choice between
life and death regarding the Mosaic law because of Ben Sira's interests in the
law of Israel, Sirach does not deny the power of human beings' free choice
under the natural law. If Sirach attributes the free choice of human beings
to the creator in the beginning, Sirach implies the existence of God's commandments from the beginning of the creation in a form of the natural law,
to which humankind can respond with free will.

Sirach 17:1–10

In Sir 17:1–10, Sirach speaks about human beings in terms of God's creation.
In this passage, the creation of humans is described in a similar way to the
Genesis account. God created human beings in his own image (17:3—"[He]
made them in his own image"; Gen 1:27—"In the image of God he created
them") out of earth (17:1a—"The Lord created human beings out of earth";
Gen 2:7—"formed man from the dust of the ground") and made them return to it again (17:1b—"and [the Lord] makes them return to it again";
Gen 3:19—"to dust you shall return"). The Lord God gave human beings
dominion over beasts and birds (17:4—"He put the fear of them in all living
beings, and gave them dominion over beasts and birds"; Gen 1:28—"have
dominion . . . over the birds . . . and over every living thing . . ."; 9:2—"The
fear and dread of you shall rest on every animal . . .") and authority over
everything on the earth (17:2; Gen 1:28). In this creation context, Sirach explains that God filled human beings with the knowledge of understanding

66. Collins, *Jewish Wisdom in the Hellenistic Age*, 60.

67. *New Oxford Annotated Bible*, 120.

68. In the first and second chapters of Romans, Paul insists that even gentiles without the law understand God's will in terms of the order of creation and, consequently,
have responsibility for their behavior. For the natural revelation in Rom 1 and 2, see
Seifrid, "Natural Revelation and the Purpose of the Law in Romans," 115–29.

and showed them good and evil (17:7). God put the fear of himself into their hearts (17:8).[69]

Through the account of the creation of human beings, Sirach reveals the natural law given to human beings in creation. They were filled during creation with the knowledge of understanding, which is found in the law of Moses as well (24:26). In 24:25–27, wisdom and understanding, which overflow from the law of Moses, are explained by way of the rivers in the garden of Eden. Ben Sira may use the rivers in Gen 2:11–14, which "flow from Eden through the world, to describe knowledge of the law flowing inexhaustibly from God through Jews to renew the spiritual life of the world."[70] Ben Sira acknowledges, however, that wisdom and understanding were given to human beings at creation too. Wisdom and understanding were created before all other things (Sir 1:4).

Natural Law in Sir 38:1–15

Ben Sira encourages the reader to honor physicians in Sir 38:1–15. The reason for this honor is explained in the first and second verses: "For the Lord created [ἔκτισεν] them; for their gift of healing comes from the Most High." A similar notion is found in Sir 38:12: "Then give the physician his place, for the Lord created [ἔκτισεν] him." Sirach 38:4 is yet another example: "The Lord created [ἔκτισεν] medicines out of the earth, and the sensible will not despise them."

Because Ben Sira proclaims that wisdom was poured upon all the Lord's works (πάντα τὰ ἔργα, Sir 1:9b), he acknowledges that God's wisdom can be found in nature through physicians and pharmacists. All the wisdom obtained from nature is God's wisdom because the Lord implanted his wisdom identified with the law in creation. Hence, the *wise* man (ἀνὴρ φρόνιμος) will not despise the medicine God created out of the earth (38:4). Sirach insists that the Lord, rather than physicians or pharmacists, created medicine. Healing's goal is returning everything to the created order. God offers skill to human beings (38:6). Regarding illness, Sirach advises one to pray to God and offer a sacrifice. And yet, he encourages, "Give the physician his place, for the Lord created him; do not let him leave you, for you need him" (38:12–13). The natural law governs the world because it is God's wisdom poured out to his works in creation. Healing by medicine is within the order of the Lord's creation. At this point, science is explained in Sirach

---

69. The rendering of NRSV, although most Greek MSS have ὀφθαλμὸν. Cf. Skehan and Di Lella, *Wisdom of Ben Sira*, 279.

70. Snaith, *Ecclesiasticus*, 125.

in terms of God's natural law. Di Lella comments concerning Sir 38:6–8: "Ben Sira encourages further study to discover other plants and herbs with medical power: the God of nature had endowed human beings with the ability to learn the mysteries of nature in order to alleviate sickness and pain."[71] Ben Sira solves the possible conflict between Judaism and Greek culture concerning healing by stating that God created doctors and medicine.[72] James Barr holds that "the reality of medicine in Ben Sira's time stimulates new developments in Hebrew thought akin to natural theology."[73]

The Order of Creation

All things are made by the Word of God, and all creatures are supposed to carry out his will. This implies that God's will is known in creation. Sirach 42:15–17 illustrates this point:

> I will now call to mind the works of the Lord, and will declare what I have seen. By the word of the Lord his works are made; and all his creatures do his will. The sun looks down on everything with its light, and the work of the Lord is full of his glory. The Lord has not empowered even his holy ones to recount all his marvelous works, which the Lord the Almighty has established so that the universe may stand firm in his glory.

Sirach 39:21 reads that everything has been created for its own purpose. Furthermore, Sir 39:31 emphasizes the obedience of nature to the Lord's command. In these verses, Ben Sira indicates that everything is under God's law, which requires obedience.

Traveling in Foreign Lands

Ben Sira supports the study of the law of the most high, which means the Mosaic law, to receive wisdom. Scribes who have much leisure and devote themselves to the study of the law of the most high will become wiser than any others involved in secular businesses (38:24–34). Ben Sira also implies, though, that wisdom can be obtained outside the law of the most high. Traveling in foreign lands is an example. Good and evil can be learned from

---

71. Skehan and Di Lella, *Wisdom of Ben Sira*, 442.

72. John G. Snaith explains this possible conflict. See Snaith, *Ecclesiasticus*, 184. For a brief introduction to Ben Sira's disputed attitude toward Hellenism, see Beentjes, "Some Major Topics in Ben Sira Research," 3–16, esp. 9–11.

73. Barr, *Biblical Faith and Natural Theology*, 179.

foreign travel (Sir 39:4). Sirach suggests that wisdom can be found in foreign lands, indicating that God's wisdom is revealed in foreign lands through the form of the natural law. Although there is no Mosaic law in foreign lands, wisdom still helps people to discern between right and wrong.

For Ben Sira, the wisdom found in foreign lands is God's wisdom as well, because "*all wisdom* is from the Lord, and with him it remains forever" (1:1). In this respect, Ben Sira seems not to have negative regard for foreign influence, unless it stands against the law of Moses or wisdom. Ben Sira might have more comfortably associated with Hellenism if he had thought that the Torah is related to the natural law in terms of God's wisdom.

As demonstrated above, Sirach shows the universality of wisdom, which existed in creation and exercises dominion over the world. This wisdom is actualized as the law of Moses. In this respect, the law of Moses can be said to have existed as unwritten law before it assigned a written form. All human beings are under the Mosaic law, whether its written form or its unwritten form. Wisdom, which is identified with the Mosaic law, can be found in foreign lands in the form of the natural law. Natural law's function is similar to that of the Mosaic law because the natural law and the Mosaic law are identical in terms of wisdom. Thus, all humans possess the responsibility for choices between life and death before God, who created wisdom in the beginning.

GENTILES UNDER THE LAW IN THE WISDOM OF SOLOMON

In addition to Sirach, the idea that gentiles are under the law can be found in the Wisdom of Solomon. An anonymous Hellenistic Jew wrote the Wisdom of Solomon, under Solomon's name, probably in the mid-second or early first-century BC.[74] The author seems to have been educated in both Jewish and Greek traditions in Alexandria, where he lived.[75]

Wisdom in the Wisdom of Solomon

In the Wisdom of Solomon, wisdom is presented "as the object of an intimate, personal religious experience, an experience that upright men enjoyed

74. Clarke, *Wisdom of Solomon*, 1–2.

75. Clarke, *Wisdom of Solomon*, 1–2. Walter T. Wilson considers the Wisdom of Solomon as one of "the most Hellenized works of the Apocrypha" because "it reflects extensive interaction with Greek literary and philosophical conventions." *New Oxford Annotated Bible*, 70.

long before the Law was given (ch 10)."[76] Although wisdom is not explicitly identified with the law of Moses in the Wisdom of Solomon, it is evident that wisdom is closely related to God's commandments as Wis 9:9 shows:

> With you is wisdom, she who knows your works and was present when you made the world; she understands what is pleasing in your sight and what is right according to your commandments [ἐντολαῖς].

Those who have wisdom can learn God's counsel and discern his will (Wis 9:13–14). Solomon prays for wisdom to learn what is pleasing to the Lord (Wis 9:10) and to be guided wisely in his actions (Wis 9:11). As David Winston mentions, Wis 9:18 infers that people need to depend on God's wisdom to achieve a righteous existence.[77] Therefore, the Wisdom of Solomon proceeds even to say that individuals are saved by wisdom (Wis 9:18).

It is significant that wisdom is not confined to the Jews but is open to anyone in God's created world. Wisdom was "from the beginning of creation" (Wis 6:22). It is the "active cause of all things" (Wis 8:5) and the "fashioner of what exists" (Wis 8:6). It "reaches mightily from one end of the earth to the other, and . . . orders all things well" (Wis 8:1). In the Wisdom of Solomon, wisdom is described with Greek philosophical vocabularies to associate "with the Logos or Pneuma, which the Stoics envisaged as a world soul."[78] Having mentioned clear Stoic overtones in 7:22—8:1, Collins aptly remarks that wisdom is associated with spirit.[79] Wisdom described as a spirit "penetrates all things" (Wis 7:24) because "she is breath of the power of God, and a pure emanation of the glory of the Almighty" (Wis 7:25). In this regard, wisdom that reveals what is pleasing to the Lord is universal. Not only Jews, but gentiles can access wisdom, too. The Wisdom of Solomon identifies wisdom with the Spirit that "has filled the world" and "holds all things together" (Wis 1:7).[80]

---

76. Reese, *Hellenistic Influence on the Book of Wisdom and Its Consequences*, 39.

77. Winston, *Wisdom of Solomon*, 208.

78. Collins, "Natural Theology and Biblical Tradition," 4. For a further explanation of Hellenistic influence on the Wisdom of Solomon, see Reese, *Hellenistic Influence on the Book of Wisdom and Its Consequences*.

79. Collins, "Natural Theology and Biblical Tradition," 4.

80. For natural theology in the Wisdom of Solomon, see Collins, "Natural Theology and Biblical Tradition," 1–15.

God, Creation, and Natural Revelation

In the Wisdom of Solomon, God is described as a creator who "created the world out of formless matter" (Wis 11:17). Human beings are also what God has made. Although the Lord created people for incorruption in the image of his own eternity, death entered the world due to the devil's envy (Wis 2:23–24). Other mention of God's creation can be found in 9:1, 2; 11:17; 13:3–5, and elsewhere.

The authority of God's judgment and destruction of the gentiles is derived from his being the creator of nations. The Wisdom of Solomon 12:12 reads:

> For who will say, "What have you done?" or will resist your judgment? Who will accuse you for the destruction of nations [ἐθνῶν] that you made [ἐποίησας]?

The judgment of gentiles is related to God being creator instead of his giving the law of Moses.

Faith in God the creator leads to the concept of natural revelation. Not knowing God and worshiping idols are criticized from the perspective of natural revelation. All people who are ignorant of God are foolish by nature (φύσει, Wis 13:1) because they fail to recognize the creator from the good things he created and instead worship creatures as gods (Wis 13:1–5). Like Rom 1:18–23, Wis 13:1–19 delineates the guilt of worshiping nature and man-made idols. Romans insists that people have known God (Rom 1:21) by natural revelation since the world's creation (Rom 1:20) and, consequently, they are without excuse (ἀναπολογήτους, 1:20) in their godless behavior. Similar ideas can be observed in Wis 13:8–9:

> Yet again, not even they are to be excused [συγγνωστοί]; for if they had the power to know so much that they could investigate the world, how did they fail to find sooner the Lord of these things?

The Wisdom of Solomon contends that humans are not free from blame if they fail to identify God the creator through creation and if, hence, they serve creatures as gods. According to the Wisdom of Solomon, gentiles are culpable due to natural revelation. Natural revelation grants gentiles some knowledge of the Lord. Natural theology, based on God as the creator, offers "Jew and Greek a common identity as citizens of the cosmos."[81] Both of them are subject to judgment depending on their behavior toward the creator.

81. Collins, "Natural Theology and Biblical Tradition," 10.

Jewish affirmation that God is the creator of the universe furnishes the reason that the Lord can judge and destroy gentiles. David Winston points to later rabbinic Judaism's use of the creation narrative to defend Israel's possession of the land of Canaan.[82] According to rabbinic Judaism, the creation narrative prevents gentiles from accusing Israel of piracy pertaining to Israel's possession of the land of Canaan.[83] God the creator is the world's owner, who can give anything to anyone with whom he is pleased.

In summary, the Wisdom of Solomon demonstrates that gentiles are under the law by explaining wisdom's universal aspect. As in Sirach, wisdom is closely related to the Mosaic law in the Wisdom of Solomon. Wisdom is found not only in Israel, but in all the nations as well, because it is the Spirit filling the world and holding all things together. Faith in God the creator and understanding natural revelation place all people under God's law and judgment. The authority of the Lord's judgment and destruction of the gentiles stems from his being the creator of the universe, who shows his wisdom in the world that he made.

GENTILES UNDER THE LAW IN BARUCH

The identification of wisdom with the Mosaic law is observed in Baruch as well. Baruch is a pseudepigraphon believed to have been written sometime between 200 and 60 BC.[84] This work consists of four sections: narrative introduction (1:1–14), prayer (1:15—3:8), wisdom poem (3:9—4:4), and Zion poem (4:5—5:9).[85] The most relevant section for this book is the wisdom poem section, Bar 3:9—4:4.

Wisdom in Baruch

Baruch's setting is the Babylonian exile. Israel's exile is described as the result of Israel sinning before God, disobeying the Lord, not heeding his voice, not obeying God's voice, not walking in God's statutes, being disobedient to him, following the intent of their own wicked hearts by serving other gods and by doing what is evil, being ungodly, doing wrong against all God's ordinances, forsaking the Lord, turning away from his law, and not

---

82. Winston, *Wisdom of Solomon*, 242.

83. Winston, *Wisdom of Solomon*, 242.

84. Biddle, "Baruch," 176.

85. Nickelsburg, "Bible Rewritten and Expanded," 140.

walking in the ways of God's commandments (1:17–22; 2:5, 8, 10, 11, 12, 24; 3:2, 4, 8; 4:12, 13).

In the wisdom poem of Baruch, however, Israel's exile is explained in terms of wisdom:

> What is it, O Israel, why is it that you are in the land of your enemies, that you are growing old in a foreign country, that you are defiled with the dead, that you are counted among those in Hades? You have forsaken the fountain of wisdom.(3:10–12)

Israel's exile is attributed to its rejection of the fountain of wisdom (cf. Jer 2:13). For restoration from the exile, Baruch, therefore, admonishes Israel to "learn wisdom" (3:9) and to "learn where there is wisdom" (3:14). Baruch then identifies wisdom with the Mosaic law: "She is the book of the commandments of God, the law that endures forever" (4:1). This identification is also hinted at in 3:29–30, which is reminiscent of Deut 30:11–13.[86] Baruch states that the Lord gave wisdom "to his servant Jacob and to Israel, whom he loved" (3:36). Having wisdom, which is the Mosaic law, is described as Israel's glory, advantages, and blessing:

> Do not give your glory to another, or your advantages to an alien people, Happy are we, O Israel, for we know what is pleasing to God.

Baruch seems to acknowledge, however, that just possessing wisdom/ the Mosaic law does not make Israel stand righteous before God. Baruch 4:1b claims, "All who hold her fast will live, and those who forsake her will die." Consequently, Bar 4:2 asks Israel to "walk toward the shining of her light" and implores, "Turn, O Jacob, and take her." Although wisdom, defined as the Mosaic law, was provided to Israel, Israel still needs to "turn" and "walk" to live. Baruch 3:12 delineates the reason for the Israelites' Exile as their forsaking "the fountain of wisdom," and then 3:13 explains the way Israel forsook it by pointing to Israel's disobedience of the law: "If you had walked in the way of God you would be living in peace forever." Baruch 3:12 and 13 demonstrate clearly that walking in the way of God is required for life rather than simply being furnished with wisdom (3:36) and knowing "what is pleasing to God" (4:4).

Baruch is found to be similar to Sirach in terms of identifying wisdom with the Mosaic law and describing wisdom to have been commanded to stay in Israel.[87] There is a significant difference between them, however, be-

86. Nickelsburg, "Bible Rewritten and Expanded," 141.

87. Whereas in Sir 24:8–12 and Bar 3:36–37, wisdom found her dwelling place in Israel, in 1 Enoch 42:1–2, wisdom returned to the heavens because she could not find

cause Baruch does not explicitly mention the universality of wisdom. While in Sirach, wisdom is described as being poured out "upon all God's works and upon all the living" (Sir 1:9, 10) and covering "the earth like a mist" (Sir 24:3), in Baruch, wisdom is not for all people. Wisdom is hidden, so that the rulers of nations cannot find the way to it and the wisest of nations fail to access it (3:15–23).[83] According to Sirach, wisdom can be found in foreign lands, so travel is encouraged for becoming wise (Sir 34:9–13, 39:4b). The scribes' wisdom is not due just to their "study of the law of the Most High (Sir 38:34)," but additionally to their seeking out "the wisdom of the all the ancients" (Sir 39:1). In Baruch, though, ancient generations did not know wisdom (3:20–21). Even in Canaan or in Teman, which were reputed for wisdom, wisdom has not been heard of (3:21).[89] The Lord chose only Israel for wisdom, and others "perished because they had no wisdom" (3:28).

God, Wisdom, and Gentiles

In Baruch, no one can have wisdom except for the Jews, whom God chose. Only Israel possesses the wisdom that is identified with the Mosaic law. Hence, the Mosaic law's relationship with the gentiles is not explicitly mentioned in Baruch. Nor is wisdom directly related to creation as in Sirach. Baruch's exclusive relating of wisdom to Israel needs to be understood with Baruch's context in mind, Israel's Exile. Although both Sirach and Baruch identify wisdom with the Mosaic law, "The tone is different because Ben Sirach wants to present an optimistic worldview, while Baruch responds to a national crisis."[90] In the exilic context, foreign nations are regarded as

---

an earthly dwelling place: "Wisdom could not find a place in which she could dwell; but a place was found (for her) in the heavens. Then Wisdom went out to dwell with the children of the people, but she found no dwelling place. (So) Wisdom returned to her place and she settled permanently among the angels."

88. Walter Harrelson's division of Bar 3:9—4:4 under seven titles is helpful in understanding the themes that Baruch presents in this part: (1) Exile due to Israel's rejection of wisdom (3 9–14); (2) The way to wisdom is hidden (3:15–21); (3) Even the wisest of nations are ignorant of wisdom (3:22–23); (4) The greatest of the ancients lacked wisdom (3:24–28); (5) God alone knows the hidden path to wisdom (3:29–36); (6) The Lord revealed wisdom to Israel (3:37–38); and (7) Wisdom identified as God's Torah (4:1–4). Harrelson, "Wisdom Hidden and Revealed according to Baruch (Baruch 3.9—4.4)," 160–62.

89. The Canaanites were the Phoenicians. The Phoenician cities of Tyre and Sidon were reputed for their wisdom. See Ezek 28:3–5 and Zech 9:2. Teman was in Edom. Its reputation for wisdom is recorded in Jer 49:7 and in Obad 1: 8–9. Moore, *Daniel, Esther, and Jeremiah*, 299. Biddle, "Baruch," 180.

90. Burkes, "Wisdom and Law," 272.

enemies in Bar 4:6, 15, 16, 25, 26, and 5:6. Baruch might not have wanted to express that the wisdom embodied as the Mosaic law in Israel can be found in other nations in the form of natural law for providing life. This mindset appears in 4:3, in which Baruch forbids Israel from giving wisdom/ the Mosaic law to the gentiles: "Do not give your glory to another, or your advantages to an alien people." Life depends on wisdom in Baruch. Thus, Israel, who has received wisdom, will eventually be delivered "from the power and hand of the enemy" (4:21). Israel's enemies, who do not know God's wisdom, will be destroyed (4:25b) as the ancient giant warriors "perished because they had no wisdom" (4:26–28). With the hope for this victory and return, Baruch seems to emphasize Israel's privileged status of possessing the Mosaic law/wisdom to the extent that no other nation has wisdom. Baruch encourages the exiled Israel, that received the Lord's wisdom, to "endure with patience the wrath" (4:25a) and utters repeatedly, "Take courage, my people/my children/O Jerusalem" (4:5, 21, 27, 30).

Although Baruch does not explicitly illustrate wisdom's universality due to the possible reasons provided above, Bar 3:32–34 still hints at the Jews' understanding of wisdom's universality by describing God, who knows wisdom, as the creator:[91]

> But the one who knows all things knows her [wisdom], he found her by his understanding. The one who prepared the earth for all time filled it with four-footed creatures; the one who sends forth the light, and it goes; he called it, and it obeyed him, trembling; the stars shone in their watches, and were glad; he called them, and they said, "Here we are!" They shone with gladness for him who made them.

Having recognized God as the creator, Bar 3:36 further states that this Lord gave wisdom to Israel, which is identified as the Mosaic law in 4:1. Since the creator God knew wisdom (Bar 3:32), God's wisdom might have worked as the natural law in his created world before it was given to Israel in the written form of the law called the Mosaic law.

In conclusion, the notion that gentiles are under the law is not clearly indicated in Baruch despite the fact that it equates wisdom with the Mosaic law as Sirach does. Unlike Sirach, Baruch does not mention wisdom's universal existence among nations as the natural law before it was given

91. Herrelson states that "Baruch's use of Sirach 24 is particularly interesting. Very little remains of the connection of Wisdom with the Creation. That part of the tradition, so central for Proverbs 8 and Sirach, is only hinted at in 3.32b-34, as the author makes what is essentially another point altogether regarding the intimate bond uniting God and Wisdom." Harrelson, "Wisdom Hidden and Revealed according to Baruch (Baruch 3.9—4.4)," 166.

to Israel as the Mosaic law. Baruch seems to emphasize wisdom's exclusive residing in Israel because of the context of Israel's Exile and the hope for return. There is still a hint at the existence of wisdom as the natural law in God's creation, though, because the Lord, who knows wisdom and gives it to Israel, is recognized in Bar 3:32–34 as the world's creator and ruler.

GENTILES UNDER THE LAW IN 4 EZRA

Fourth Ezra is the next text to be considered with regard to gentiles being under the law. Fourth Ezra is also included as the third through the fourteenth chapters of 2 Esdras in the Apocrypha of English Bibles.[92] It is believed to have been written during the last decade of the first century, or about AD 100.

Gentiles being under the Mosaic law is not always explained in terms of wisdom in Hellenistic Judaism. As mentioned above, Baruch does not explicitly connect wisdom, which is identified with the Mosaic law, to gentiles in the concept of the natural law, although one may identify the hidden idea of wisdom's universality in Bar 3:32–34. Likewise, 4 Ezra does not employ the wisdom tradition to place gentiles under the law of God. Nevertheless, 4 Ezra reveals the idea that gentiles have been aware of the Mosaic law from the beginning.

The Law Approved by All

In 4 Ezra, the law is depicted as a gift from God to Israel (4 Ezra 3:19; 9:31–32).[93] Fourth Ezra 5:27 also describes the Lord giving the law to Israel. Israel's possession of the law is due to God's love and the election of Israel (4 Ezra 5:23–27). What is intriguing about the statement of giving the law to Israel is that God "has given the law which is approved by all" (4 Ezra 5:27). Michael Stone recognizes that this verse seems to be an implication that all human beings approve the Torah.[94] If all humans endorse the law, it must have been known to them all in a certain way. For Jacob Myers, this verse indicates that all nations have the law, although Israel has the best.[95]

---

92. For the introduction to 4 Ezra, see Metzger, "Fourth Book of Ezra," 517–24.

93. For other themes, such as God, humanity, epistemology, and death in 4 Ezra, see Burkes, *God, Self, and Death*, 159–233.

94. Stone, *Fourth Ezra*, 131.

95. Myers, *I and II Esdras*, 193.

God's Giving of the Law to Human Beings

How did gentiles know the law, which they approved and which was given to Israel? Fourth Ezra 7:21 says that God gave his law to all human beings living on earth:

> For God strictly commanded those who came into the world,
> when they came, what they should do to live, and what they
> should observe to avoid punishment.

The Lord's commandment was offered not only to the Jews but to all "who came into the world, when they came." Michael E. Stone contends that this verse refers to people in general, and is not limited to Israel.[96] All individuals know God's law from birth by nature. For him, the plural form of "my statutes" in 4 Ezra 7:11, which Adam transgressed, is also a term "usually indicating the Torah or divine commandments in general and not the specific command given to him."[97] In 4 Ezra 7:20, an angel says to Ezra, "Let many perish who are now living, rather than that the law of God which is set before them be disregarded!" This claims that God's law is established before all human beings, including gentiles. Fourth Ezra 7:20 and 21, which refer to people in general, are reminiscent of Deut 30:15, which was given to Israel: "See, I have set before you today life and prosperity, death and adversity." The law of the Lord is set before all human beings, Jews and gentiles.

Freedom to Choose between Life and Death

Obedience to the law is the means of avoiding death for Jews and gentiles alike. As Shannon Burkes mentions, each individual who receives the law "makes a choice and bears the responsibility for his actions."[98] All who come into the world are required to choose between life and death. In 4 Ezra, life and death depend on people's attitude toward the law, i.e., obedience or disobedience. Fourth Ezra 3:8 states, however, that "every nation walked after its own will and did ungodly things" before God. This statement is like Rom 3:9–11 and 23, which testify to the sinfulness of all humankind. Gentiles should have obeyed the Lord's commandment to walk after his will. In 4 Ezra 3:8, Ezra again implies that God's will was revealed to every nation with the expectation of its obedience. It followed its own will, though, rather than God's will. Every nation has the freedom to choose between the

96. Stone, *Fourth Ezra*, 194–95.

97. Stone, *Fourth Ezra*, 194.

98. Burkes, "'Life' Redefined," 58.

Lord's will and its own will. Fourth Ezra 8:55–56 explains the freedom that humankind received:

> Therefore do not ask any more questions about the multitude of those who perish. For they also received freedom, but they despised the Most High, and were contemptuous of his Law, and forsook his ways.

The words "freedom" and the "law" can be found in this text. Gentiles have the freedom to obey the law. They perish because they are contemptuous of the law given to them.

Evil Heart and the Law

One of the characteristics of 4 Ezra is its frequent use of the figure of Adam (3:5–7, 10, 21; 4:30; 6:54, 56; 7:11, 70, 116, 118).[99] The concept of the *yetzer ha-ra'* appears in 4 Ezra with regard to Adam.[100] Adam was burdened with an evil heart (4 Ezra 3:21). According to 4 Ezra 4:30, "A grain of evil seed was sown in Adam's heart from the beginning," and it has produced ungodliness. All Adam's descendants do as he did because they have an evil heart too (4 Ezra 3:26). This evil disposition is an obstacle when people try to obey the law. Ezra wonders why God did not remove the evil heart from Jacob's descendants and the posterity of Israel when he gave the law and commandment to them, so that the "law might bring forth fruit in them" (4 Ezra 3:19–20). The law and the evil root stay together in the people's heart (4 Ezra 3:22) and stand against each other.

Fourth Ezra seems to maintain that the law, which is supposed to suppress the evil heart, though, was present even in Adam and his descendants. Having stated that God did not take away the evil heart from Israelites so that the law might bring forth fruit in them, Ezra seems to find in Adam and his descendants examples of the conflict between the evil heart and the law:

> For the first Adam, burdened with an evil heart, transgressed and was overcome, as were also all who were descended from him. Thus the disease became permanent; the law was in the people's heart along with the evil root, but what was good departed, and the evil remained . . . This was done for many years;

99. For a detailed discussion concerning Adam in early Judaism, see Levison, *Portraits of Adam in Early Judaism*. Adam in 4 Ezra is included in the seventh chapter of his book (113–27).

100. Desjardins finds an early form of the *yetzer ha-ra'* in 4 Ezra. Desjardins, "Law in 2 Baruch and 4 Ezra," 33.

> but the inhabitants of the city transgressed, in everything doing
> as Adam and all his descendants had done, for they also had the
> evil heart. (4 Ezra 3:21–26)

Adam is seen as the first instance showing that law could not bring forth fruit because of the evil heart. Not only Adam but all his descendants transgressed because they possessed the evil heart as well. Although the law has been "in the people's heart," Adam's descendants "transgressed" as Adam did. Ezra is likely to affirm that the law could not function properly ever since Adam's time due to the inherent evil heart. Because the conflict between the law and the evil heart is the reality of all human beings born after Adam, all humans have the law in them as the countering force of the evil heart.[101] Ezra indicates that not only Jews, who have the Mosaic law, but all human beings suffer the same conflict.

Judgment of Gentiles by the Law

In 4 Ezra, gentiles are judged because of the law. This sheds light on gentiles' being under the law as well. According to 4 Ezra 7:37, gentiles will be judged because they despise God's commandments:

> Then the Most High will say to the nations that have been raised
> from the dead, "Look now, and understand whom you have de-
> nied, whom you have not served, whose commandments you
> have despised!"

Paul Brooks Duff provides insightful interpretation regarding this verse. First of all, he understands "the nations" as referring to gentiles. He then asserts that "gentiles had access to the Law of God because otherwise the phrase 'whose commandments you have despised' makes no sense."[102] According to Duff, this text states that gentiles will be condemned before God because they had access to the Torah, but rejected it.

Fourth Ezra 13:37–38 indicates that gentiles will be judged by the law:

> And he, my Son, will reprove the assembled nations for their un-
> godliness (this was symbolized by the storm), and will reproach
> them to their face with their evil thoughts and with the torments
> with which they are to be tortured (which were symbolized by

---

101. Michael P. Knowles understands the law to be a good *yetzer*, or impulse, in 4 Ezra. Knowles, "Moses, the Law, and the Unity of 4 Ezra," 270.

102. Duff, "Glory in the Ministry of Death," 324.

the flames); and he will destroy them without effort by the law
(which was symbolized by the fire).[103]

The "Son" in 13:37 refers to the Messiah.[104] Messiah is described as
a judge in this text. As M. A. Knibb observes, the law is the standard by
which Messiah exercises judgment.[105] In addition, this text is reminiscent
of Rom 2:15–16, in which Christ appears as a judge with God to judge gentiles according to the law written in their hearts. For Michel Desjardins, in
4 Baruch, law is a measuring stick against which gentiles are judged and
destroyed.[106]

Fourth Ezra 7:72 also affirms that those who dwell on earth will be
judged by the law:

> For this reason, therefore, those who dwell on earth shall be
> tormented, because though they had understanding they com-
> mitted iniquity, and though they received the commandments
> they did not keep them, and though they obtained the Law they
> dealt unfaithfully with what they received.

The reason for their judgment is that they did not keep the commandments and the law, which were given to them. Although they had understanding, they committed iniquity. They are without excuse because of this
as 4 Ezra 7:73 (cf. Rom 1:20) reads, "What, then, will they have to say in the
judgment, or how will they answer in the last times?" Fourth Ezra shows
that gentiles are under the law and, consequently, condemned by the law
when they disobey it.

In brief, although 4 Ezra depicts the law as a gift given to Israel by God,
the law is not understood as the commands to which only Israel is subject.
All human beings approved the law, which remained in their hearts as the
opposite force against evil hearts. According to 4 Ezra, all who come into the
world possess God's law. As a result, God's law will judge all of them for life
or death. Gentiles are under the law as much as Jews are.

---

103. Bruce M. Metzger's translation and parentheses. Metzger, "Fourth Book of
Ezra," 552.

104. Explicit reference to Messiah as "my son" is found in 4 Ezra 7:28–29: "For my
son the Messiah shall be revealed with those who are with him . . . my son the Messiah
shall die . . ." The messianic phrase, "my son," is additionally observed in 13:32, 52 and
14:9. Although Michael Edward Stone uses "my servant," rather than "my son," in his
translation of 13:37, Metzger and Myers prefer "my son." Metzger, "Fourth Book of
Ezra," 552; and Myers, *I and II Esdras*, 305.

105. Coggins and Knibb, *First and Second Books of Esdras*, 267.

106. Desjardins, "Law in 2 Baruch and 4 Ezra," 35.

GENTILES UNDER THE LAW IN 2 (SYRIAC APOCALYPSE OF) BARUCH

Second Baruch is another Hellenistic Jewish source in which is found the idea that gentiles are under the law too. Second Baruch is a pseudepigraphon, originally written in Palestine in Hebrew, which was later translated into Greek. The Syriac Apocalypse of Baruch is translated from Greek.[107] Although this text presents itself as having been prompted by Jerusalem's destruction in 587 BC, it is commonly believed that 2 Baruch was composed after AD 70, most likely in the first or second decade of the second century.

Unwritten Law and Written Law

Chapter 57 of 2 Baruch states that there was unwritten law at the time of Abraham and his sons, that is, before the coming of the Mosaic law. Second Baruch 57:2 reads:

> For at that time the unwritten law was in force among them, and the works of the commandments were accomplished at that time, and the belief in the coming judgment was brought about, and the hope of the world which will be renewed was built at that time, and the promise of the life that will come later was planted.

The works of the commandments were able to be accomplished because of the unwritten law even before the time of Moses, through whom the law was given to Israel. Belief in the coming judgment is based on unwritten law as well. According to Desjardins, the reference to the "unwritten law" in 2 Bar 57:2 "reveals that those who came before Moses also had access to God's word."[108]

After mentioning the "unwritten law," 2 Baruch covers the coming of Moses and the law in chapter 59. Although the explicit words the "written law" are not employed in this chapter, given the fact that chapter 57 refers to "unwritten law," the law coming at the time of Moses in chapter 59 can be recognized as the "written law." The coming of the Mosaic written law is illustrated as the light illuminating in darkness (59:2). This illumination of the Mosaic law is described, however, as the work of "the lamp of the

107. For the introduction to 2 Baruch, see Klijn, "2 (Syriac Apocalypse of) Baruch," 615–20.

108. Desjardins, "Law in 2 Baruch and 4 Ezra," 28.

eternal law."[109] The lamp of the law exists forever and ever, illuminating all people in darkness. The Mosaic law's eternal existence asserted in 59:2 may explain why 2 Baruch could claim that the works of the commandments were accomplished at the time of Abraham, the son of his son, and "those who are like them" (57:1). In this regard, the unwritten law—which existed before the Mosaic law's illumination—is not utterly different from the law of Moses in 2 Baruch

"One Law by One"

In 2 Baruch, God is one who is identified as the creator of the universe.[110] According to Baruch, Israel "received one Law from the One" (48:24). At the end of 2 Baruch, he again declares that "there is one Law by One, one world and an end for all those who exist" (85:14). If there is one God and one law, it could be warranted that the unwritten law and the written law are one law coming from one God, the creator of the world. Baruch says that there is one world. The Jewish nation and gentile nations are not different in terms of creation and judgment. The Lord created one world, which is subject to his judgment according to one law. All people living in the "one world" of God are under his "one law."

Wisdom, Law, and Creation

Law is related to wisdom and intelligence in 2 Baruch (51:3, 4). To stop hearing the law is tantamount to stop hearing wisdom and to stop receiving intelligence (51:4). Second Baruch 38:2–4 identifies law with wisdom, implying that associating with the law is the same as possessing wisdom. Second Baruch 48:24 mentions law as excellent wisdom too. Law is identified with wisdom in 77:16 as well. As a result, those who know the law are considered to be "wise and understanding" (46:5). Israel is advised to obey them with fear to learn the law.

109. Law is frequently identified with light and lamp in 2 Baruch. So, Moses' bringing the law is depicted as lighting a lamp to Israel (17:4). When Baruch leaves the people, they worry that there would be no light among them (46:2). But later, in 78:15, Baruch assures them that the law providing lamp will abide, even though people leave. If they look upon the law, the lamp will not be wanting (78:16); J. Edward Wright conjectures that the author of 2 Baruch places Baruch, and actually himself through Baruch, in the same position of authority as Moses in providing the law ("lamp") and interpreting the law. See Wright, "Social Setting of the Syriac Apocalypse of Baruch," 81–96.

110. God is implied or mentioned as the creator in 2 Bar 10:19; 14:15, 17; 17:4; 21:4–7, 25; 24:4; 78:3; 79:2; 82:2; 85:2, 3.

Wisdom and understanding, though, which are related to the law, can be found in God's creation as well. In this respect, 2 Bar 48:9–10 states:

> You instruct the creation with your understanding, and you give wisdom to the spheres so that they minister according to their position. Innumerable hosts stand before you and serve peacefully your sign according to their positions.

Because God's wisdom and understanding are revealed in his creation, anyone who does not learn from it becomes unrighteous, as 2 Bar 54:17–19 indicates:

> But now, turn yourselves to destruction, you unrighteous ones who are living now, for you will be visited suddenly, since you have once rejected the understanding of the Most High. For his works have not taught you, nor has the artful work of his creation which has existed always persuaded you. Adam is, therefore, not the cause, except only for himself, but each of us has become our own Adam.

God's works and the artful work of his creation provide understanding and persuade people to righteous living. Frederick J. Murphy correctly observes the thrust of this verse when he comments that "creation itself manifests God's ways, and any careful observer of creation will find and worship God."[111] In 2 Bar 54:13–14, when God is mentioned as creator, he is also confessed as the one who "established the whole fountain of light"[112] and "prepared under [his] throne the treasures of wisdom."

Adam cannot be reproved for his descendants' sins because all of them receive God's understanding through the works of his creation, and choose for themselves (54:15). Thus, Baruch stresses individual responsibility, saying that "each of us has become our own Adam." Although Baruch acknowledges that "Adam sinned first and has brought death" (54:15), he delineates individual ability to choose by portraying Adam "as the paradigm of the choice of both evil and good."[113]

---

111. Murphy, "Sapiential Elements in the Syriac Apocalypse of Baruch," 315.

112. As already mentioned, law is frequently identified with light and lamp in 2 Baruch.

113. Levison, *Portraits of Adam in Early Judaism*, 137. In 4 Ezra, death is more directly attributed to Adam (3:7; 7:118). However, 4 Ezra affirms individual responsibility as well. See 122–25 of Levison's *Portraits of Adam in Early Judaism*. On the other hand, it is interesting to observe that Sirach blames Eve for the death of human beings: "From a woman sin had its beginning, and because of her we all die" (Sir 25:24).

Gentiles' Judgment and the Law

Judgment is expressed in terms of the law and understanding in 2 Bar 15:5–6. The reason for man's understanding of God's judgment is explained by the fact that they received the law and understanding:

> It is true that man would not have understood my judgment if he had not received the Law and if he were not instructed with understanding. But now, because he trespassed, having understanding, he will be punished because he has understanding.

Man is punished because he trespasses with understanding. Eckhard J. Schnabel assumes that "man" refers to Israel because he feels that "Israel is clearly presented as recipient of the Torah" in 32:1; 44:3, 7; 46:4–5; and 77:3, 15–16, and that the author's general intention is showing "the liability of the Jews (not of gentiles) with regard to their knowledge of the law."[114] Schnabel may be correct in his recognition of the author's purpose for writing 2 Bar. This passage, however, seems to reveal the general principle, which can be applied to both Jews and gentiles, that all humans are able to understand guilt in God's judgment because of the law and understanding that they received. Second Baruch 48:39–40 furnishes a similar idea, but—in this case—the man who understands being guilty before the judge is "each of the inhabitants of the earth."

> Therefore, a fire will consume their thoughts, and with a flame the meditations of their kidneys will be examined. For the Judge will come and will not hesitate. For each of the inhabitants of the earth knew when he acted unrighteously, and they did not know my Law because of their pride.[115]

Second Baruch implies that no one is ignorant of God's law because the Lord's creation witnesses his law in terms of understanding and wisdom. Everyone can understand being guilty in God's judgment because of the law and understanding given to him by the Lord.

Second Baruch's concept of natural law has already been touched on above by presenting some relevant verses of 2 Baruch. This concept, however, can also be found in 2 Bar 14:17, 21:4–5, and 48:45–47. It is stated in 2 Bar 14:17 that God devised and spoke by means of his Word to make the

---

114. Schnabel, *Law and Wisdom from Ben Sira to Paul*, 155.

115. In 2 Bar 48:32, the phrase "all inhabitants of the earth" appears in relation to judgment, which A. F. J. Klijn regards as referring to nations. See the section of "nations" in Klijn, "2 (Syriac Apocalypse of) Baruch," 619.

works of his creation. In 2 Bar 21:4–5, the Lord is again described as the creator, who demands obedience according to his law:

> O hear me, you who created the earth, the one who fixed the firmament by the word and fastened the height of heaven by the spirit, the one who in the beginning of the world called that which did not yet exist and they obeyed you. You who gave commandments to the air with your sign and have seen the things which are to come as well as those which have passed.

God gave commandments to his creation, and it obeyed him. Therefore, sin is not only the transgression of God's law, but neglecting to recognize the Lord as the creator as well (48:46).

Second Baruch, thus, indicates that the unwritten law was in force among those who lived before the time of Moses. It functioned like the Mosaic law among them. The Mosaic law, which is light in darkness, came as the written law among the Jews. There is, however, only one law in one world, which is given by one God. God the creator "established the whole fountain of light" in his creation and "prepared under [his] throne the treasures of wisdom," which are identified with the law. All people are under God's one law, which is illuminating as the natural law and the Mosaic law. Second Baruch asserts that gentiles can understand the Lord's judgment because they received God's law.

GENTILES UNDER THE LAW ACCORDING TO PHILO OF ALEXANDRIA

The concept that gentiles are additionally under the law can be found in Philo of Alexandria, who is a contemporary of Jesus and Paul. Philo of Alexandria (ca. 20 BC–AD 50) was an intellectual Jew living in Alexandria.[116] He endeavored to present the law of Moses "in a way acceptable to Hellenistic thinking."[117]

Mosaic Law and the Law of Nature

Philo considers the Mosaic law as closely related to the law of nature: "But Moses is alone in this, that his laws, firm, unshaken, immovable, stamped, as it were, with the seals of nature herself, remain secure from the day when

---

116. For a brief introduction to Philo and a related bibliography, see Evans, *Ancient Texts for New Testament Studies*, 167–73.

117. Borgen, *Philo of Alexandria: An Exegete for His Time*, 10.

they were first enacted to now" (*Mos.* 2.14).[118] Because the law of Moses is stamped with the seals of nature, it represents "the purpose and will of nature" (*Opif.* 3)

In addition, the Mosaic law is congruent with Greek virtues, such as "love of humanity, of justice, of goodness, and hatred of evil" (*Mos.* 2. 9–11). The Mosaic law is a manifestation of Greek virtues.[119]

Philo's treatise *De Opificio Mundi* sheds light on his understanding of the law and nature relationship. According to *De Opificio Mundi* 3, the way to be a loyal world citizen is to observe the law of Moses. The Mosaic law represents nature's purpose and will and, therefore, keeping the law is regulating one's life according to the purpose and will of nature. In this respect, Philo could say that "the world is in harmony with the Law, and the Law with the world" (*Opif.* 3).

As we have seen already, Philo recognizes that Moses began his law book with the description of the creation of the universe to show two things: (1) "The Father and Maker of the world was in the truest sense also its Lawgiver"; and (2) "he who would observe the laws will accept gladly the duty of following nature and live in accordance with the ordering of the universe" (*Mos.* 2:48). For Philo, as Peder Borgen insists, "Mosaic law comes from the One God" who is the "Creator and Lawgiver."[120]

Patriarchs and the Law

Although Moses delivered Israel the law on Mount Sinai, for Philo, it was already in force among the patriarchs. Philo maintains in *De Abrahamo* 276 that Abraham obeyed the law: "Such was the life of the first, the founder of the nation, one who obeyed the law."[121] Philo's statement is likely to be an echo of Gen 26:5, which testifies that Abraham kept "my charge, my commandments, my statutes and my laws."[122] Philo already has written in

---

118. All Philo's texts are derived from *Philo with an English Translation*, LCL, 10 vols.

119. David M. Hay points out two characteristics of Philo's interpretation of the individual Pentateuch laws: Philo's emphasizing tendency of (1) "their relation to the Law of Nature," and (2) "their manifestation of the primary Greek virtues." Hay, "Philo of Alexandria," 373.

120. Borgen, *Philo of Alexandria*, 148. See 144–53 of his book for more information on the Mosaic law and cosmic law.

121. Sirach also similarly claims that Abraham obeyed the Mosaic law: "He kept the law of the Most High, and entered into a covenant with him" (Sir 44:20).

122. ‏מִשְׁמַרְתִּי מִצְוֹתַי חֻקּוֹתַי וְתוֹרֹתָי:‏, MT/ τὰ προστάγματά μου καὶ τὰς ἐντολάς μου καὶ τὰ δικαιώματά μου καὶ τὰ νόμιμά μου, LXX.

De Abrahamo 275 that Moses said regarding Abraham "that this man did the divine law and the divine commands" (ὅτι τὸν θεῖον νόμον καὶ τὰ. θεῖα προστάγματα). Translators of Philo attach a footnote referring to Gen 26:5 here thinking Philo has that text in mind.[123]

Philo believes that Abraham kept the law not because of written words, but due to unwritten nature: "He did them, not taught by written words, but unwritten nature gave him the zeal to follow where wholesome and untainted impulse led him" (*Abr.* 275). In this regard, Philo concludes his *De Abrahamo* by calling Abraham himself "a law and an unwritten statute" (*Abr.* 276).[124]

According to Hindy Najman, Philo recognizes the Mosaic law to be in agreement with the pre-Sinaitic law, that is, the law of nature and, consequently, it is available to all who use reason.[125] Patriarchs embodied the law, becoming the living law and νόμοι ἔμπψυχοι.[126] Philo thought that patriarchs could have obeyed the Mosaic law, even before it was given to Israel, through living in conformity with nature:

> For in these men we have laws endowed with life and reason, and Moses extolled them for two reasons. First he wished to shew that the enacted ordinances are not inconsistent with nature; and secondly that those who wish to live in accordance with the laws as they stand have no difficult task, seeing that the first generations before any at all of the particular statutes was set in writing followed the unwritten law with perfect ease, so that one might properly say that the enacted laws are nothing else than memorials of the life of the ancients, preserving to a later generation their actual words and deeds. For they were not scholars or pupils of others, nor did they learn under teachers what was right to say or do: they listened to no voice or instruction but their own: they gladly accepted conformity with nature, holding that nature itself was, as indeed it is, the most venerable of statutes, and thus their whole life was one of happy obedience to law . . . . (*Abr.* 5–6)

123. Philo, *Philo with an English Translation*, vol. 6, LCL 289, 135. Philo, *Works of Philo*, 434.

124. Hindy Najman mentions *b. Yoma* 28a and *m. Qiddushin* 4:14 as similar instances in rabbinic traditions, in which Abraham was claimed to have *fulfilled* or *performed* the commandments. Najman, "The Law of Nature and the Authority of Mosaic Law," 66n34.

125. Najman, "Law of Nature and the Authority of Mosaic Law," 62 and n. 24 on the same page.

126. Calabi, *Language and the Law of God*, 3.

Unwritten Law and Written Law

Hence, the concept of written law and unwritten law is found in Philo. The written law of Moses is a copy of the unwritten law of nature. His comprehension of the relationship between written law and unwritten law seems to be influenced by "Platonic dualism, in which the visible and sensible world of changing matter is taken to be a copy of an invisible, immaterial universe of 'ideas.'"[127] In addition, his perspective on the law of nature is understandable in light of the Stoic concept of the law of nature.[128] Although unwritten law and written law are different in their way of existence, they possess the same origin: God, the creator.

The unwritten law in Greek thought "can refer to the uncodified customs of a people or a law, or laws, which are considered universal, but uncodified."[129] Additionally, in Philo, it refers to the wise people living according to the law of nature.[130] Although Naomi Cohen holds that Philo refers to the oral law of the rabbis with his statement of unwritten law, it is rejected by many—including John W. Martens, Hindy Najman, and David M. Hay.[131] In Philo, the written law of Moses is a true copy of God's eternal unwritten law which nature reveals. There is no one without the law. Both Jews and gentiles are under the law. For Philo, there is only one law given by one God, even though the form of existence is different.

In summary, according to Philo, the natural law and Mosaic law are not different from each other. The Mosaic law represents nature's purpose and will. In this respect, the Mosaic law is a copy of the natural law under which the world operates. Those who live in conformity with nature's unwritten law are the living law, just as the patriarchs were. For Philo, it can be said that Abraham obeyed the Mosaic law, which is available to all who employ reason. God is the world's creator and lawgiver. His law existed as the unwritten law even before it assumed written form, becoming the Mosaic law.

127. Barclay, *Jews in the Mediterranean Diaspora*, 164. Barclay claims that "Philo's thought is structured by Platonic dualism."

128. Najman, "Law of Nature and the Authority of Mosaic Law," 57.

129. Martens, "Philo and the 'Higher' Law," 313.

130. Martens, "Philo and the 'Higher' Law," 314–16.

131. Cohen, "Jewish Dimension of Philo's Judaism," 165–86. For the criticism on Cohen's view, see Martens, "Unwritten Law in Philo," 38–45; Najman, "Law of Nature and the Authority of Mosaic Law," 68; and Hay, "Philo of Alexandria," 376.

GENTILES UNDER THE LAW IN PSEUDO-PHILO'S *BIBLICAL ANTIQUITIES*

Pseudo-Philo's *Biblical Antiquities*, which is frequently called *Liber Antiquitatum Biblicarum* according to its Latin title, is yet another place that the notion that gentiles are also under the law can be identified. Pseudo-Philo's *Biblical Antiquities* was composed in the first century, probably at about the time of Jesus in Palestine.[132]

In 11:2 of *Biblical Antiquities*, God speaks to Moses regarding the function of the law:

> I will put my words in your mouth, and you will enlighten my people, for I have given an everlasting Law into your hands and by this I will judge the whole world. For this will be a testimony. For even if men say, "we have not known you, and so we have not served you," therefore I will make a claim upon them because they have not learned my Law.[133]

According to this text, the law given to Moses is intended to be a standard by which the Lord judges the entire world. Not only the Jews but also the gentiles are subject to God's judgment to be performed according to the law of Moses. Pertaining to this text, Paul B. Duff correctly explains that "God indicated that it [law] was intended not just for Israel but for all."[134]

Biblical Antiquities 32:7 shows that the Mosaic law is connected with the world's creation:

> And when their enemies had dealt with them wickedly, the people cried out to the Lord, and their prayer was heard, and he brought them out of there and brought them to Mount Sinai and brought forth for them the foundation of understanding that he had prepared from the creation of the world . . . .

It is intriguing that the text indicates that God had prepared the Mosaic law from the world's creation. Although this verse does not explicitly mention the Mosaic law's existence before Sinai, it seems to imply that the Mosaic law existed from the creation of the world.

132. Harrington, "Pseudo-Philo," 299–300.

133. Harrington, "Pseudo-Philo," 318.

134. Duff, "Glory in the Ministry of Death," 324.

CONCLUSION

Do gentiles have nothing to do with the Mosaic law, which was given to Israel on Mount Sinai? With this question in mind, we have explored in this chapter some Hellenistic Jewish sources and have discovered that Hellenistic Judaism places gentiles under the law. Jewish sources such as Sirach, the Wisdom of Solomon, Baruch, 4 Ezra, 2 Baruch, Philo of Alexandria, and Pseudo-Philo show the Mosaic law's universal validity.

Although Hellenistic Jews recognized the Mosaic law as the ethnic privilege which God gave them because of his love and election, they connect the Mosaic law to all nations with various methods. Sirach relates the Mosaic law to the natural law by way of wisdom. The Mosaic law is the embodiment of wisdom (Sir 24:8, 11, 12), which exists "over every people and nation" (Sir 24:6). Wisdom identified with the Mosaic law can be found in foreign lands and therefore, gentiles there can discern between good and evil. While the Mosaic law is the written form of the wisdom, the wisdom found in foreign lands can be considered as the unwritten form of the Mosaic law. This concept of unwritten law preceding the written law can be observed in Greek thought as well. Wisdom embodied to Israel as the Mosaic law transcends the boundary of Israel and existed before the coming of the Mosaic law.

Wisdom of Solomon depicts wisdom as the Spirit, which fills the world and holds all things together (Wis 1:7). Thus, wisdom closely related to the Mosaic law can be found in all nations. Although Baruch restricts the wisdom identified with the law within the boundary of Israel, this phenomenon can be understood from the perspective that Israel was exiled and hoping for return by its enemies' destruction due to their having "no wisdom" (Bar 3:28). However, even in Baruch, the Jews' understanding of wisdom's universality is hinted at when Baruch describes God as the creator who knows wisdom (Bar 3:32–36).

In addition to Hellenistic Judaism's concept of wisdom, its view of God as creator plays an important role in placing all nations under the law of God and his judgment. God is the creator (2 Bar 54:13–14), and his wisdom and understanding are revealed in his creation (2 Bar 54:18). Thus, anyone who does not learn from it ends up being unrighteous (2 Bar 54:17). All his creation obeys him according to his law (2 Bar 21:4–5). The judgment of gentiles by the Mosaic law is attested in 4 Ezra 7:37, 72 and 13:37–38.

In 4 Ezra, the Mosaic law given to Israel is the law "approved by all" (4 Ezra 5:29). All human beings were commanded by God when they came into the world "what they should do to live, and what they should observe to avoid punishment" (4 Ezra 7:21). Thus, all individuals know God's law from birth by nature.

Philo connects the Mosaic law to the law of nature. The Mosaic law represents "the purpose and will of nature" (*Opif.* 3). Thus, keeping the law is regulating one's life according to the purpose and will of nature. Patriarchs, including Abraham, could keep the law due to their living in conformity with nature (*Abr* 5, 6, 276). For Philo, the written law of Moses is a copy of the unwritten law of nature.

There are similarities between the idea of natural law in Sirach and Greek ideas of the law. However, it cannot be said that the Jewish idea of natural law originated from Hellenism. According to Menahem Kister, "The Second Temple period was, above all, the period of interpretation, and its major project was amalgamating, through interpretation, concepts from diverse biblical strata in a Hellenistic environment."[135] Ben Sira's idea of the natural law might have been his new interpretation of the Jewish concept of the natural law in a Hellenistic environment, with his understanding of wisdom and God the creator.

The idea of the natural law and faith in God the creator was presumably functioning in Hellenistic Judaism to resolve the tension between Judaism and Hellenism in terms of morality. The concept of natural law embodied as the Mosaic law might have been the ground from which the Mosaic law could claim itself as a norm for Hellenistic world ethics.

135. Kister, "Wisdom Literature and Its Relation to Other Genres," 19.

CHAPTER 3

Gentiles under the Law in Romans

INTRODUCTION

LARRY R. HELYER ASSERTS that "it should not be forgotten that the NT it-self is a product of Second Temple Judaism. As Christians, we all too often forgot the larger context in which it emerged."[1] Considering his insightful comment, it is no wonder that Paul, a Hellenistic Jew, places gentiles under the law in similar ways to other Hellenistic Jewish authors as seen in chapter 2. Gentiles being under the Mosaic law is not an absurd idea to the Hellenistic gentiles nor to Hellenized Jews.

Paul places gentiles under the Mosaic law to prove their moral failure before God. Although they did not receive the written law of Moses, they cannot contend that they did not know it because the Mosaic law is the natural law's embodiment, which they have possessed since the world's creation. Paul's seemingly contradictory theology that lawless gentiles are under the Mosaic law can be viewed as legitimate by considering the idea of the written law and the natural-law concept in Hellenistic Judaism's literature.

In this chapter we shall examine Romans to see that Paul explains his gospel from the perspective that gentiles not having the law are under

1. Helyer, *Exploring Jewish Literature of the Second Temple Period*, 23. Chris Van-Landingham similarly states, "One must understand the Apostle Paul's letters within the greater context of the Greco-Roman world and, in particular, within the religious environment of Early Judaism." VanLandingham, *Judgment and Justification in Early Judaism and the Apostle Paul*, 1.

the law and its condemnation. Paul's soteriology, therefore, can be properly understood when we follow his characteristic way of presenting gentiles as under the law and its judgment in this letter. It is hoped that this investigation sheds light on Paul's understanding of the law and gentiles.

ROMAN 1:18–32: GENTILES IN FOCUS

In Rom 1:18—3:20 Paul talks about the universal sinfulness of human beings.[2] Having proclaimed in 1:17 the righteousness of God revealed in the gospel, Paul shows the sinfulness of human beings and the resulting condemnation in 1:18—3:20. The righteousness of God can be understood as two kinds of righteousness, namely, judging righteousness and saving righteousness. In order to explain the saving righteousness, the judging righteousness of God needs to be placed and explained first.[3] Since God is righteous, he reveals his wrath against "all ungodliness and unrighteousness" and judges those who do such things. Romans 1:18–32 belongs to Paul's indictment of human beings, which continues to 3:20.[4]

It has been debated whether Paul's indictment in 1:18–32 is directed to both Jews and gentiles or only to gentiles. Some argue that the indictment is universalized to include both Jews and gentiles.[5] Their argument is based on the alleged echoes of Israel in verses 23–24 (Ps 106:20, Jer 2:11), alleged echoes of Adam in verses 20–22, 25 (Gen 3), Paul's use of ἀνθρώπων rather than ἔθνη in verse 18, and the relationship between 1:18–32 and 2:1.[6] However, a more convincing argument, which is also traditional, is that gentiles are in focus in 1:18–32. This argument is based on: the comparison between this passage and 2:1—3:8 (thinking Jews are the focus in the latter passage); idolatry being considered the sin of gentiles by the Jews; homosexual relations being not uncommon among the gentiles; allusions to Ps 106:20 and Jer 2:11; and Paul's idea to apply them to the gentiles, etc.[7] Furthermore,

2. Bell, *No One Seeks for God*, 11.

3. In this regard, Schreiner well titles Rom 1:18–3:20 with the words "God's Righteousness in His Wrath against Sinners." Schreiner, *Romans*, 77.

4. Schreiner regards Rom 3:21—4:25 as the part dealing with "the saving righteousness of God." Schreiner, *Romans*, 176–244.

5. Bell, *No One Seeks for God*, 94–95.

6. Hooker, "Adam in Romans I," 297–306; Frid, "How Does Romans 2.1 Connect to 1.18–32?," 109–30; Jewett, *Romans*, 160–62; Caneday, "'They Exchanged the Glory of God for the Likeness of an Image,'" 34–45.

7. Fitzmyer, *Romans*, 269–77; Schreiner, *Romans*, 77–82; Not providing any argument, John Murray also agrees that this passage "deals with the sin, apostasy and degeneration of the Gentile world." Murray, *Epistle to the Romans*, 35.

Mark A. Seifrid disagrees with those who find echoes of Israel and Adam in this passage.[8] Regarding the alleged echo of Ps 106:20 ("Thus they exchanged their glory for the image of an ox that eats grass") in Rom 1:23, Seifrid contends that Paul "follows Genesis 1:20–25 (which provides him with the sequence πετεινά,, τετράποδα, ἑρπετὰ.), and not Psalm 106:20 (which speaks of the worship of the 'calf')." He also points out the different wording between Paul and the psalm: "the exchange of the likeness of the calf for the true God" in the Psalm and "the exchange of the image of God for the likeness (of the image) of the mortal human being" in Paul.

Regarding the alleged echo of Adam, Seifrid points out that "Adam did not perceive the things of God through the created order, he walked with the Lord God in the Garden" and that while people in Rom 1 claim themselves to be wise, Adam was tempted "to *acquire* 'the knowledge of good and evil.'"[9] Although it is true that Jews are also under the natural revelation and made an idol in the wilderness, Paul seems not to focus on Jews in this passage. Perhaps the most significant reason for thinking this way is the fact that Paul employs the concept of the natural law/revelation rather than the Mosaic law for his indictment. Moo also points out this fact in his argument that this passage refers mainly to gentiles:

> The knowledge of God rejected by those depicted in 1:18–32 comes solely through "natural revelation"—the evidence of God in creation and perhaps, the conscience. The situation with Jews is, of course, wholly different, for Paul holds them responsible for the special revelation they have been given in the law (cf. 2:12–13, 17–29).[10]

Paul seems neither to indict Israel directly nor allude to Adam in this text. Paul's focus is on gentiles.[11] In this passage Paul puts gentiles under the wrath and judgment of God.[12]

8. Seifrid, "Unrighteous by Faith," 117–18.

9. Seifrid's italics.

10. Moo, *Epistle to the Romans*, 97.

11. I. Howard Marshall notes, "In the remainder of Romans 1 the focus is clearly on the Gentiles." Marshall, *New Testament Theology*, 308.

12. Having understood that "verses 1:18–32 speak primarily about Gentiles," Peter Stuhlmacher titles this part as "1:18–32. Gentiles under the Wrath of God." Stuhlmacher, *Paul's Letter to the Romans*, 33; according to Timo Laato, Paul indirectly refers to Sapientia Salomonis in Rom 1:18–32. Laato, *Paul and Judaism*, 85, 87–89.

GENTILES UNDER THE LAW IN ROM 1:18–32

In this passage it can be observed that Paul puts gentiles under the law. Although they did not receive the Mosaic law on Mount Sinai, for Paul they are under it by their knowledge of God, which is available through natural revelation and natural law.

Despite the fact that gentiles do not have the Mosaic law (Rom 2:14), according to Paul, they are "without excuse" (ἀναπολογήτους [Rom 1:20]) for suppressing the truth by their wickedness (1:18), and consequently are under the wrath of God. The grounds for their being under the wrath of God without excuse are explained by Paul in terms of the concept of natural revelation and natural law in this passage.

In verse 19, Paul claims that "what can be known about God is evident ἐν αὐτοῖς" because God has shown it to them. God is depicted here as the provider of certain divine knowledge, as he gave the Mosaic law to Israel. This knowledge is not only available to gentiles but also evident ἐν αὐτοῖς. Regarding the meaning of ἐν αὐτοῖς, scholars have different views such as "to them,"[13] "among them,"[14] or "in them."[15] The question raised from these various renderings of ἐν αὐτοῖς is whether it refers to the conscience, mind, or heart of each person ("in them"), or refers to each group of people ("among them" or "to them").

Having realized this question, Robert Jewett decides to "make the ambiguous translation 'within them'" regarding ἐν αὐτοῖς.[16] His rendering, however, seems not to be neutral, as he intended originally, between "in them" and "among them," because other scholars such as Joseph Fitzmyer consider "within them" to be equivalent to "in them," both of which imply people's inner faculties.[17] The immediate context composed of verses 19 and 20 appears to be in favor of "among them" or "to them." However, verses 26, 27, and particularly 32 seem to support the view of "in them" as well. Therefore, both "among them" and "in them" seem to fit well with Paul's argument and thus do not necessarily exclude each other. Paul is likely affirming gentiles' knowledge of God by pointing to the revelation of the visual nature among them (v. 20) and the witness of the invisible nature such as conscience and natural order in them (vv. 26, 27).

---

13. Morris, *Epistle to the Romans*, 80; Fitzmyer, *Romans*, 279; Bell, *No One Seeks for God*, 38.

14. Moo, *Epistle to the Romans*, 103.

15. Calvin, *Epistle of Paul the Apostle to the Romans and to the Thessalonians*, 31.

16. Jewett, *Romans*, 153.

17. Fitzmyer, *Romans*, 279.

Furthermore, by saying ἐν αὐτοῖς, Paul seems to emphasize the closeness of the knowledge of God to gentiles. What can be known about God is present *in* and *among* them. It is not far from them. It is readily available within their touch. This idea reminds us of Paul's argument in Rom 10:5–8, where he employs Deut 30:12–14 to prove that Christ and the word are close to all human beings just as the Mosaic law was close to the Jews. In Deut 30:11–14, Mosaic law is claimed to remain close to the Jews, so that they can obey it:

> "For this commandment which I command you today is not too difficult for you, nor is it out of reach. It is not in heaven, that you should say, 'Who will go up to heaven for us to get it for us and make us hear it, that we may observe it?' Nor is it beyond the sea, that you should say, 'Who will cross the sea for us to get it for us and make us hear it, that we may observe it?' But the word is very near you, in your mouth and in your heart, that you may observe it." (NASB)

The closeness of the law to the Jews is emphasized by various expressions such as "nor is it out of reach," "not in heaven," "nor is it beyond the sea," "is very near you," "in your mouth," and "in your heart." This nearness entails the obedience of the Jews as implied in such expressions: "is not too difficult for you," "who will go up to heaven . . . that you may observe it?" "who will cross the sea . . . that we may observe it?" and " . . . that you may observe it." Likewise, in Rom 1:19–20, the closeness of the knowledge of God to gentiles, which is emphasized by the expression ἐν αὐτοῖς, entails the gentiles' proper response to God. This closeness of the Mosaic law and the knowledge of God makes Jews and gentiles respectively without excuse. Whereas Jews cannot say that "we needed someone who might have gone up to heaven or down to the sea to get the law," gentiles cannot say that "we did not know about God," since the knowledge of God was ἐν αὐτοῖς. Romans 1:20 explicitly says that gentiles are without excuse.

Gentiles' possession of the knowledge of God is due to God's initiative in making it known. Romans 1:19 affirms that it is God who has shown the knowledge of himself to gentiles ("for God has shown it to them," ὁ θεὸς γὰρ αὐτοῖς ἐφανέρωσεν). The conferrer of the Mosaic law to Jews and the knowledge of God to gentiles are the same God, who is the creator of the universe. Thus Jews do not need to make someone search for the law through heaven and the sea, because God has already given the written book of the law to the Jews (Deut 30:10). Gentiles do not need to undergo "a long process of reasoning" to know God, because God revealed himself to them (v. 19b).[18]

18. Schreiner, *Romans*, 86: "To understand that Paul does not refer to a long process

Although gentiles did not receive the written form of the Mosaic law, they are nevertheless not without the knowledge of God. They have it ἐν αὐτοῖς as close as the Jews have the law in their mouths and hearts.

As James Dunn acknowledges, "some sort of natural theology" can be found in 1:19–20.[19] In verse 20 Paul states that a knowledge of God is available by natural revelation. His invisible things (τὰ. . . . ἀόρατα αὐτοῦ) such as his eternal power and deity can been seen (καθορᾶται) and understood when gentiles look at things he has made. Paul's use of oxymoron in τὰ . . . ἀόρατα αὐτοῦ/ . . . καθορᾶται seems to be intentional.[20] God's *invisible* things became *visible* and understandable to gentiles through what is created. Thus, gentiles cannot argue that they did not respond to God because they could not see him. Paul's seemingly intentional oxymoron ends up in his assertion that "they are without excuse." Whereas the written law of Moses was given to the Jews on Mount Sinai, the knowledge of God, which is available through natural revelation, has been given to all human beings ever since God's creation of the world (ἀπὸ κτίσεως κόσμου, 1:20).[21] In Paul there was no time when the knowledge of God was unavailable to gentiles despite their lack of the Mosaic law. Since gentiles know God, they are required to respond to God appropriately by honoring, thanking, and worshiping him as God (1:21–25).

Then, what is the knowledge of God which Paul thinks to be available to gentiles by natural revelation? What kind of knowledge of God makes gentiles without excuse in Paul's mind? What kind of truth are the gentiles suppressing, thereby remaining under the wrath of God (1:18)? In verse 19, what gentiles can obtain is "what can be known about God (τὸ γνωστὸν τοῦ θεοῦ)." In verse 20, it is "his invisible things," that is, "his eternal power and deity." In verse 21, the object of the knowledge is "God" (γνόντες τὸν θεὸν). As scholars generally explain, the knowledge of God, which gentiles received by natural revelation, may be God's existence and nature.[22] However, the knowledge Paul has in mind seems to be extended to the knowledge of the will of God. In 1:21–31, Paul condemns gentiles because of their

---

of reasoning by which people come to a knowledge of God's existence and power is critical. God has stitched into the fabric of the human mind his existence and power, so that they are instinctively recognized when one views the created world."

19. Dunn, *Romans 1–8*, 56.

20. This oxymoron has been observed by many scholars such as Cranfield, Fitzmyer, and Moo. Cranfield, *A Critical and Exegetical Commentary*, 114; Fitzmyer, *Romans*, 280; Moo, *Epistle to the Romans*, 105. Cranfield thinks it to be intentional.

21. In the words ἀπὸ κτίσεως κόσμου, ἀπὸ has a temporal meaning rather than indicating source. Moo, *Epistle to the Romans*, 105n64; Byrne, *Romans*, 73.

22. Moo, *Epistle to the Romans*, 105

behavior against the will of God despite of their knowledge of God (1:21) and his ordinance (1:31). In this regard, Seifrid is correct in his statement, "Paul's further argument reveals that he regards the created order as imparting not only a knowledge of God the creator, but a knowledge of his will."[23] Gentiles' knowledge of God is "full and sufficient" knowledge for them to worship God as creator.[24] After having listed gentiles' sins from 1:21 to 1:31, Paul boldly proclaims in 1:32 that "they know the ordinance of God (τὸ δικαίωμα τοῦ θεοῦ), that those who practice such things are worthy of death (ἄξιοι θανάτου)."

Homosexuality is mentioned as a representative sin of gentiles against God's will in verses 26 and 27. The reason for Paul's criticism of this behavior is expressed by the words "exchanged the natural (φυσικὴν) function for that which is unnatural (παρὰ φύσιν)"(v.26) and "abandoned the natural (φυσικὴν) function" (v.27). Cranfield understands φυσικός to mean "in accordance with the intention of the Creator" and παρὰ φύσιν to mean "contrary to the intention of the Creator."[25] Using the word "natural," Paul here claims that same-sex relations are contrary to the will of God. "Nature" here means God's created order or the concept of natural law rather than individual character or disposition.[26] Gentiles know by their nature that homosexuality is against the intention of God in his creation. They violate the will of God not because of their ignorance but because of their "degrading passions," to which God gave them over because of their idolatry. Verses 26 and 27 shows that gentiles have the knowledge of God's will by the natural law, which is in the hearts of human beings.

In verse 32, gentiles' knowledge of God is expanded even to the knowledge of the moral norms of the Mosaic law. Paul states in verse 32 that "they know the ordinance (δικαίωμα) of God." The word δικαίωμα is used by Paul again in 2:26 and 8:4 in his reference to the Mosaic law. It seems, therefore, that Paul has in mind the Mosaic law in his use of δικαίωμα in 1:32.[27] If that is the case, then it follows that Paul means, in this verse, that gentiles have the knowledge of the ordinance of the Mosaic law. What gentiles know

23. Seifrid, "Natural Revelation and the Purpose of the Law in Romans," 120.

24. Seifrid, "Natural Revelation and the Purpose of the Law in Romans," 119.

25. Cranfield, *Romans 1–8*, 125.

26. Hays, "Relations Natural and Unnatural," 194–97; Schreiner, "A New Testament Perspective on Homosexuality," 65–69.

27. Thielman states regarding δικαίωμα that "when it occurs elsewhere in the New Testament to mean 'regulation,' 'requirement' or 'commandment,' as it does here, always refers to the Mosaic law (Lk 1:6; Rom 2:26; 8:4; Heb 9:1, 10)." Thielman, *Paul and the Law*, 169. Cf. Schreiner, *Romans*, 140. Bell, however, thinks δικαίωμα refers to "the principle of retribution." Bell, *No One Seeks for God*, 61.

about the ordinance of God is expressed after the ὅτι that "those who practice such things are worthy of death." Although gentiles did not receive the Mosaic law, Paul seems to consider that they know it from the natural law in their hearts. Schreiner also understands Paul in this way saying regarding 1:32 that "Gentiles, without specifically having the Mosaic law, are aware of the moral requirements contained in that law."

Thielman's suggestion about the implication of "death" in 1:32 unfortunately has not received much attention among commentators. He finds here the echo of Deut 30:15 and 19, where life and death were set before the Jews to choose.[28] The Mosaic law determines life and death according to the works of the law. Likewise, in Paul's thought, gentiles are under the judgment between life and death according to their works of the ordinance, which is also known to them. Although James D. G. Dunn finds an Adamic background in this verse ("In the day you eat of it you shall die" [Gen 2:16]), his interpretation is not convincing since the vice list in Rom 1:29–31 cannot be applied to Adam.[29] Interestingly, Grant R. Osborne, agreeing with Dunn, argues that verse 32 may allude to the Gen 2—3 story of the death penalty because "the vice list of verses 29–31 were not worthy of death."[30] But he seems to miss the point Paul is making. Paul clearly maintains that "those who practice *such things* are *worthy of death*" (οἱ τὰ τοιαῦτα πράσσοντες ἄξιοι θανάτου εἰσίν). Although it may not be acceptable, according to any civil code, to claim the death penalty based on the vice list of verses 29–31, especially, being full of envy, arrogant, boastful and disobedient to parents, etc., nevertheless, it cannot be rejected that Paul connects the sins listed in verses 29–31 to the death penalty according to God's law. Thielman conjectures that Paul might have "linked the penalty of death referred to in Deuteronomy 30:15, 19 to the sinful attitudes listed in 1:29–31" because "Deuteronomy 30:17 envisions obedience from the heart."[31]

Both the word "ordinance" implying the Mosaic law and "death" echoing Deut 30:15 and 19 denote that Paul puts gentiles under the law and its condemnation. Gentiles are aware of the moral norms of the Mosaic law.

28. Thielman, *Paul and the Law*, 169.

29. Dunn, *Romans 1–8*, 69 and particularly 76.

30. Osborne, *Romans*, 58.

31. Thielman, *Paul and the Law*, 290n32.

GENTILES' JUDGMENT ACCORDING
TO WORKS IN ROM 2:6-11

Romans 2:6–11 shows that God's judgment will be performed according to works. Paul claims in 2:6 that God will render to every man according to his works (κατὰ τὰ ἔργα αὐτοῦ). In verse 7 "eternal life" is promised to those who do good (ἔργου ἀγαθοῦ), seeking for glory, honor, and immortality. Verses 9 and 10 show that God's judgment depends on whether one *does* evil (κατεργαζομένου τὸ κακόν, v.9) or *does* good (ἐργαζομένῳ τὸ ἀγαθόν, v.10). This principle of judgment by works is applicable both to Jews and gentiles as Paul mentions at the end of verses 9 and 10: "of the Jew first and also of the Greek (Ἰουδαίου τε πρῶτον καὶ Ἕλληνος, v. 9)" and "to the Jew first and also to the Greek (Ἰουδαίῳ τε πρῶτον καὶ Ἕλληνι, v. 10)." God judges both Jews and gentiles by the same criterion, that is, works, because he is impartial (2:11).[32]

The priority of Jews in judgment is demonstrated by the words "Jews first." It implies, as Schreiner aptly points out, that "the special privilege of the Jews involves greater responsibility."[33] Jews have greater responsibility in doing good, because they boast in God (καυχᾶσαι ἐν θεῷ, 2:17) and in law (ἐν νόμῳ καυχᾶσαι, 2:23); they know the will of God by being instructed out of the law (2:18); they are confident that they are guides to the blind, a light to those who are in darkness (2:19), correctors of the foolish, and teachers of children (2:20, cf. 2:21 and 22). However, they do not live up to their privilege. While gentiles do not honor (οὐχ . . . ἐδόξασαν) God as God despite their knowledge of him (1:21), Jews dishonor (ἀτιμάζεις) God through their breaking of the law in which they boast (2:23). Having the law is surely a privilege of Israel (Rom 9:4). However, simply having the law without keeping it does not make Israel better than gentiles. As Francis Watson rightly observes, the purpose of verses 6–11 is "to contradict the view that God will bestow eternal life on Jews (cf. vv. 7,10), whereas Gentiles who do not have the law and circumcision will be condemned (cf. vv. 8, 9)."[34] Paul claims in 2:6 that God will render to every man according to *his works* (κατὰ τὰ ἔργα

---

32. For a good investigation of God's impartiality in Romans, see Bassler, *Divine Impartiality*, esp. 121–70, and Bassler, "Divine Impartiality in Paul's Letter to the Romans," 43–58. Although Paul emphasizes God's impartiality in 2:6–11, divine impartiality is not likely the main theme in this passage, nor in the entire book of Romans. Schreiner and Witherington, against Bassler, regard divine impartiality simply to be a supporting element for Paul's main thesis such as "God is righteous in his judging Jews who violate his commandments" or "there is no excuse before God's judgment." Schreiner, *Romans*, 113. Witherington III with Hyatt, *Paul's Letter to the Romans*, 150.

33. Schreiner, *Romans*, 114.

34. Watson, *Paul, Judaism, and the Gentiles*, 200.

αὐτοῦ) rather than simply having the written form of Mosaic law or being in covenant relationship with God. Judgment according to works, however, has already been proclaimed to the Jews in Ps 61:13 LXX (κατὰ τὰ ἔργα αὐτοῦ, 62:13 MT; 62:12 ET) and Prov 24:12 (κατὰ τὰ ἔργα αὐτοῦ) as Seifrid points out.[35]

In Rom 2:6–11, although Paul puts Jews first before God's judgment, which will be accomplished according to works, he does not fail to include gentiles in that same judgment. God's judgment is impartial because it will be applied not only to Jews but also gentiles by the same criterion, that is, their works. Paul goes on to explain in Romans 2:12–16 the standard by which God judges Jews' and gentiles' behavior. The standard Paul presents is the Mosaic law. Paul puts gentiles as well as Jews under the Mosaic law in Rom 2:12–16, and claims that gentiles know the Mosaic law without receiving the written law of Moses. In Paul's theology, Jews and gentiles will be judged according to the works reckoned by the Mosaic law.

GENTILES UNDER THE LAW IN ROM 2:12–16

Paul's notion that lawless gentiles are under the law is observed in Rom 2:12–16 because he says here that gentiles as well as Jews will be judged according to their doing of the Mosaic law.

In Rom 2:12 Paul makes a distinction between Jews and gentiles in terms of their possession of the law: (1) all who have sinned without the law, and (2) all who have sinned under the law. N. T. Wright correctly identifies the sinners without the law as gentiles and the sinners under the law as Jews.[36] Despite this clear difference, Paul speaks of the equal condemnation of Jews and gentiles. Lawless gentile sinners will *perish* (ἀπολοῦνται) without the law just as law-given Jewish sinners will be *judged* (κριθήσονται) by the law. According to Moo, there is "no distinction in meaning between ἀπόλλυμι and κρίνω . . . in this verse," because ἀπόλλυμι is frequently used in the Scriptures "to depict the results of a negative verdict in the eschatological judgment (e.g., Pss. 9:5; 37:20; 1 Cor. 1:18, 19; 8:11; 15:18; 2 Cor. 2:15; 4:3; 2 Thess. 2:10)."[37] Jews and gentiles, therefore, have no difference in terms of the result of their sin in spite of the difference in possessing the written law of Moses.

35. Seifrid, "*Romans*," 611.

36. Wright, *Letter to the Romans*, 440; Morris understands law in v. 12 to be "the law of Moses." Morris, *Epistle to the Romans*, 122.

37. Moo, *Romans*, 146n13 and 14

In verse 12, Paul does not provide any reasons why gentile sinners not having the law will perish, whereas for Jews he mentions the law as the standard by which they will be judged. Nevertheless, Paul at least makes it clear that gentiles are not free from condemnation on the pretext of not having the written law of Moses. They also perish when they sin as Jews do. As asserted in Romans chapter 1, Paul here again affirms that gentiles are without excuse about their sins.

Verses 14–16 are very intriguing, because Paul, who did not speak in verse 12 about the standard by which gentile sinners will "perish"—equivalent to "being judged" now proceeds to relate lawless gentiles with the Mosaic law using the natural law concept.[38] We have already seen a similar phenomenon in Rom 1:18–32. Paul accuses gentiles, who do not have the Mosaic law, of their sinfulness in the light of natural law and revelation in Rom 1:18–27. Having enumerated additional vice lists in verses 29–31, he pronounces the death penalty to those who do such sins, alluding to the Mosaic law in Rom 1:32. Gentiles' judgment is explained in terms of the Mosaic law.[39] Here in Rom 2:14–16 we find again that Paul puts lawless gentiles under the judgment of the Mosaic law, which is available to gentiles by the natural law.

In verse 14, Paul states that gentiles do by nature the things of the law (φύσει τὰ τοῦ νόμου ποιῶσιν). "The law" here means the Mosaic law.[40] "The things of the law" is understood by scholars as "what the law prescribes"[41] or "some of the precepts of the law."[42] By "the things of the law," Paul is likely referring to the moral norms of the Mosaic law. It is clear that gentiles do not keep the Sabbath, feasts, and food laws by nature. It is also clear that the law which gentiles keep excludes circumcision in 2:26 and 27.

Having observed no definite article preceding ἔθνη, commentators understand ἔθνη to be "'some Gentiles,' not necessarily all Gentiles."[43] Mat-

38. Schreiner rightly points out that the νόμος "in verses 12–15 refers to the Mosaic law." Schreiner, *Romans*, 118.

39. Bell contends that "although he [Paul] had already shown in 1.18–32 that the Gentiles deserve death, he has not explicitly explained the criteria by which the Gentiles will be judged." However, Paul seems to refer to Mosaic law as the criterion in 1:32 by using the term δικαίωμα and by alluding to "death" in Deut 30:15 and 19 as we have already discussed. Bell, *No One Seeks for God*, 146.

40. Black, *Romans*, 48.

41. Hodge, *A Commentary on Romans*, 55.

42. Fitzmyer, *Romans*, 309.

43. Fitzmyer, *Romans*, 309. Similarly, Mounce comments that "Paul was speaking about *some* Gentiles, not *all* Gentiles" (italics original). Mounce, *Romans*, 94n97. In addition, Leon Morris notes that "it is not the Gentiles as a whole that Paul has in mind here, but people who have the quality of being Gentiles." Morris, *The Epistle to the*

thew Black, who considers ἔθνη "*some* Gentile nations," states, "The absence of the article is significant: '*The* Gentiles' would mean all or most Gentile nations. But Paul would hardly concede that *the* Gentiles do naturally what the law enjoins—some Gentile nations certainly, and even this is subsequently qualified."[44]

However, ἔθνη in verse 14 should not be understood to imply that only *some* gentiles know the law of God and obey it. Distinguishing the meaning between *some* and *all* based on the presence or absence of the definite article before the word ἔθνη seems arbitrary. Charles Hodge claims that "this word has, without the article, in virtue of its frequent occurrence, a definite sense," referring to Rom 3:29, 9:24 and 30.[45] Furthermore, Paul's intention of mentioning gentiles who do the things of the law is to indicate that gentiles without the written law also have the law by which they will be judged. Any gentiles, virtually all gentiles, can do the things of the law by nature and show that they have the works of the law written in their hearts (Rom 2:15). Hodge, therefore, seems to be correct in stating:

> As ἔθνη is without the article, many would render it *heathen*, that is, *some heathen*. But in the first place, it is evident from the context that this is not what the apostle means to say. His object is to show that the heathen world have [*sic*] a rule of duty written on their hearts; a fact which is not proved by some heathen obeying the law, but which is proved by the moral conduct of all men. Men generally, not some men, but all men, show by their acts that they have a knowledge of right and wrong.[46]

After all, in verse 14 Paul seems to denote the possibility that gentiles, more specifically any gentiles, can do what the Mosaic law prescribes, having the knowledge of it.

In verse 14, ὅταν ("when" or "whenever") can also be interpreted as Paul's implication of the possibility of gentiles doing the Mosaic law by nature: "*when* gentiles who do not have the law do the things of the law by nature." For John W. Martens, however, ὅταν means "if" rather than "when" or "whenever."[47] He argues that Paul makes a conditional argument with ὅταν. In other words, Paul does not believe that there are any gentiles who do the law. Paul's argument is based on "if," that is, if there are any gentiles who do the law, although it is unlikely. Martens' interpretation is the result of

---

Romans, 124. So also Cranfield, *Romans 1–8*, 155n3.

44. Black, *Romans*, 47–48. Italics original.

45. Hodge, *Commentary on Romans*, 55.

46. Hodge, *Commentary on Romans*, 54–55. Italics in original.

47. Martens, "Romans 2:14–16," 63.

his effort to solve the seemingly contradictory statements in Paul. For him, verse 14 appears incompatible with Paul's other statements such as those which reveal salvation being possible by Christ alone and "negative view of the capabilities of Jews and the law of Moses."[48] He denies thus the reality of gentiles doing the law by interpreting ὅταν to be "if." Although Martens provides some significant insights regarding interpretation of verse 14–16 in terms of Stoic reading, he fails to grasp Paul's intention in mentioning gentiles doing the things of the law in this passage. Paul does not intend to prove that there are some gentiles who will be saved by doing the law. What Paul is arguing for here is that Jews' mere possession of the law is not an advantage because gentiles also have the law despite lacking the written law of Moses, and they do it occasionally.[49] Possessing the Mosaic law is not the sign of salvation for Paul since gentiles also have heard the law written on their hearts. Paul uses the case of gentiles to instruct Jews that obedience of the law is required for justification, rather than possession of it. Paul, therefore, mentions in this passage the *reality* of gentiles doing the law despite not having the written law of Moses by placing them paradoxically under it by employing the natural law concept, which Martens also finds using the Stoic theory of the law of nature.[50] As James Dunn rightly comments, Paul implies "the reality, not just hypothetical possibility" of gentiles doing the law. Ernst Käsemann, who understands ὅταν to be "whenever," mentions that Paul's statement is related to his experience.[51] By means of ὅταν Paul implies that occasional obedience to the Mosaic law can be found among gentiles due to their being aware of the law in them.

Although some scholars including Cranfield argue that φύσει is linked with ἔχοντα making the sense that "Gentiles which *do not possess the law by nature*,"[52] it is more likely to be connected with ποιῶσιν meaning that "Gentiles *do by nature* the things of the law."[53] Had Paul wanted φύσει to be connected with ἔχοντα, according to Dunn and Fitzmyer, he would have put it before ἔχοντα as in Rom 2:27, Gal 2:15, and Eph 2:3.[54]

---

48. Martens, "Romans 2:14–16," 60.

49. See Schreiner, "Did Paul Believe in Justification by Works?," 144–47.

50. Martens, "Romans 2:14–16," 64–67.

51. Käsemann, *Commentary on Romans*, 62.

52. Cranfield, *Critical and Exegetical Commentary on the Epistle to the Romans*, 156–57. Other supports include Maertens, "Une étude de Rm 2.12–16," 510–11; Jewett, *Romans*, 214.

53. Supporters of this view are Bruce, *Romans*, 86; Dunn, *Romans 1–8*, 98; Fitzmyer, *Romans*, 310.

54. Dunn, *Romans 1–8*, 98; Fitzmyer, *Romans*, 310.

Gathercole argues against Dunn, Fitzmyer, and Bell by citing some examples of φύσει occurring at the end of a phrase or after a verb: Wisdom of Solomon 13.1, Ignatius' *Letter to the Ephesians* 1.1, Josephus' *Jewish Antiquities* 8.152.[55] Based on these citations, he maintains that "it does demonstrate that many scholars have assumed the standard position without any foundation." However, scholars seem to prefer to connect φύσει to ποιῶσιν from Paul's own usage of φύσει found in his texts, such as in Rom 2:27, Gal 2:15, and Eph 2:3. Paul's usage of φύσει in his own letters seems to be a more significant foundation than other authors' examples in judging Paul's use of φύσει in Rom 2:14.

Moreover, when we consider Paul's use of the natural law/revelation concept in Romans chapter 1 and Hellenistic Judaism's understanding of the natural-law concept, it is more likely that Paul employs the same concept here again to demonstrate that gentiles also have the law and *do it by nature* despite their lack of the written law of Moses. Stuhlmacher supports this view saying "by virtue of their [gentiles] having been created according to the standard of wisdom (which according to Sir. 24:23ff. is manifest in the Law), they themselves can by all means declare what is good and evil."[56] Moo also understands Paul to be implying "unwritten" or "natural" law concept, which is widespread in Greek tradition.[57]

Lawless gentiles' possession of the law is articulated by Paul in this expression: οὗτοι νόμον μὴ ἔχοντες ἑαυτοῖς εἰσιν νόμος ("these not having the law are the law to themselves"). Paul uses the word νόμος two times here, that is: (1) these not having the *law*, (2) they are the *law* to themselves. The first law clearly refers to the Mosaic law. Then, what does the second νόμος refer to? Fitzmyer believes that Paul uses it in a figurative sense to refer to "human nature."[58] Moo considers it to be used as "an extended sense," denoting "the 'demand of God' generally."[59] However, with the second νόμος Paul is likely to refer to the Mosaic law as well, thereby making the following sense: Gentiles, who do not have the Mosaic law, are actually the Mosaic law to themselves. Herman Ridderbos represents this view, saying "indeed, they are, by so doing, a law to themselves, namely, *that one specific law* (Rom. 2:14, 15)."[60] He attaches a footnote to this statement that "Gutbrod justly writes: 'If [*nomos*] without article implied here a generalization of the

55. Gathercole, "Law unto Themselves," 35–36.

56. Stuhlmacher, *Paul's Letter to the Romans*, 43.

57. Moo, *Epistle to the Romans*, 150.

58. See Fitzmyer, *Romans*, 310, and the introduction section about "the law" in 131.

59. Moo, *Epistle to the Romans*, 151.

60. Ridderbos, *Paul*, 106. Italics mine.

concept of law, the train of thought would be broken' (TDNT, IV, p. 1070)."[61] Paul's purpose in Rom 2:14–16 is to prove that gentiles also have the Mosaic law to debunk the Jews' false idea that mere possession of the Mosaic law stands them righteous before God. Although Paul acknowledges that gentiles do not have the written law of Moses, he claims that gentiles have the Mosaic law by stating that gentiles themselves are the Mosaic law in a sense. Then he explains in what sense gentiles are the Mosaic law to themselves in the following verses by employing the words "conscience" and "the work of the law written in their heart."[62] Therefore the second νόμος in verse 14 can be better understood as referring to the Mosaic law rather than human nature or some other universal law.[63] By using human nature and natural law concept, Paul states that gentiles are the Mosaic law to themselves. Paul's intention is to correct the Jews' wrong idea that they are the only people who have the Mosaic law and that possession of the law can make themselves righteous before God even without doing it.

Gentiles having the Mosaic law is explained in verse 15. Paul states that the "work of the law" is written in gentiles' hearts. According to Schreiner, the "work of the law . . . refers to the commands contained in the Mosaic law."[64] Although they do not have the written law of Moses, they are not ignorant of it, since the work of the law is written in their hearts. Some scholars contend that this expression of Paul signifies the fulfillment of Jer 31:33 (Jer 38:33 LXX), where God promises to write his law on his people's hearts in the new covenant era.[65]

This interpretation leads them to believe the gentiles in view here to be gentile Christians.[66] However, Rom 2:15 is more likely to refer to the unbelieving gentiles as Mark A. Seifrid contends.[67] He argues against the gentile Christian view by pointing out that (1) Paul speaks of the *work* of the law written *in* their hearts rather than the *law* written *upon* their hearts,

---

61. Ridderbos, *Paul: An Outline of His Theology*, 106–107n36. Dunn also argues that "indeed the whole point of what Paul is saying here would be lose if νόμος was understood other than as a reference to *the* law, the law given to Israel." Dunn, *Romans 1–8*, 99. Italics original.

62. A similar understanding can be found in Dunn. See Dunn, *Romans 1–8*, 99.

63. Dunn states regarding the second νόμος that "it is not some other universal or 'unwritten law' . . . which Paul has in view." Dunn, *Romans 1–8*, 99.

64. Schreiner, *Romans*, 122.

65. Cranfield, *Romans 1–8*, 158–59; Jewett, *Romans*, 215.

66. Cranfield, *Romans 1–8*, 159; Jewett, *Romans*, 213.

67. Seifrid, *Christ, Our Righteousness*, 53. So also Moo, *Epistle to the Romans*, 152. For a more detailed explanation, see Schreiner's *Romans*, who also concludes that this passage has unbelieving gentiles in view. Schreiner, *Romans*, 121–24.

and (2) Paul mentions the accusation that some of them will receive by their thoughts at the day of judgment (2:15). For Schreiner, Romans 2:15 "does not specifically quote or necessarily allude to Jer. 31:33 (38:33 LXX)" to show "a saving work of God."[68] Here Paul's purpose is to demonstrate that gentiles also "*know* what the law commands" by employing "the popular Greek conception of a natural law written on the heart."[69] The "work of the law" (Rom 2:15) along with the "things of the law" (Rom 2:14), which gentiles do by nature, refer to what the Mosaic law demands.[70] Gentiles have the Mosaic law, presumably its moral norms, written in their hearts, and this fact is witnessed by the function of the conscience in them (Rom 2:15). Paul seems to connect the Mosaic law with the natural law, since he explains gentiles being the Mosaic law to themselves by means of the natural law concept, which can be detected in Paul's expressions such as doing the things of the law by nature, work of the law written in the hearts, and conscience.

Romans 2:15–16 shows the standard of gentiles' judgment. It is the work of the law written in their hearts. Gentiles will be equally judged as the Jews according to the Mosaic law, although the form of the law differs between them: for Jews it is the written law of Moses, whereas for gentiles it is the unwritten law or the natural law, which is identified with the Mosaic law in Hellenistic Judaism. Gentiles are the Mosaic law to themselves. For Paul, who is a son of Hellenistic Judaism, gentiles also know the moral norms of the Mosaic law in the light of natural law and revelation. In this sense, Paul puts gentiles under the Mosaic law along with the Jew in his explanation of the gospel. Gentiles are equally sinners in the light of the Mosaic law. It is the embodiment of the unwritten law of God which is available to all human beings.

The work of the law written in the hearts of gentiles, and their consciences and thoughts accusing or excusing (ἀπολογουμένων, Rom 2:15) remind us of Paul's previous reasoning about natural revelation in Rom 1:18–20 that gentiles are "without excuse" (ἀναπολογήτους, Rom 1:20) because gentiles have known God since the creation of the world through the natural revelation. As Paul addresses in Rom 1:20 that the knowledge of God is communicated by creation, he maintains in Rom 2:15 that the will of God is written on the hearts of gentiles in his creation and they can do it by nature.

Although gentiles can be *outwardly* categorized as people without the law (Rom 2:12a, 2:14a, cf. 2:28), in Paul's theological reasoning especially

---

68. Schreiner, *Romans*, 122.

69. Schreiner, *Romans*. Italics in original.

70. Moo, *Epistle to the Romans*, 151.

in relation to the condemnation and redemption of gentiles, they can be considered *inwardly* to be under the Mosaic law. Mosaic law is substantially identical with the natural law in terms of the giver, that is, God the creator, and the function of it, namely, conveying the will of God and leaving people without excuse.

For Paul, the creator God is the only God who deserves the glory both from Jews and gentiles (Rom 1:18–25), and who makes it happen, when people impinge on his glory, that "all who have sinned without the law will also perish (ἀπολοῦνται) without the law, and all who have sinned under the law will be judged by the law" (Rom 2:12). Gentile sinners without the law are also under the judgment of the law and perish. Moo is, therefore, basically correct in his statement that there is "no distinction in meaning between ἀπόλλυμι and κρίνω" in Rom 2:12: Gentile sinners will perish, Jewish sinners will be judged. Why gentiles will perish (ἀπόλλυμι) is explained in verse 16 in light of Christ's judgment act according to the work of law written in their hearts.

ROMANS 3:19

In Rom 3:19 Paul states that "Now we know that whatever the law says, it speaks to those who are in the law (ἐν τῷ νόμῳ), in order that every mouth (πᾶν στόμα) might be closed (φραγῇ) and all the world (πᾶς ὁ κόσμος) be held guilty (ὑπόδικος) before God."[71] Regarding this passage, A. B. Caneday points out that "of the various significant issues that exegetes address, in this text, one that receives too little attention is the inner logic of verse 19."[72] Then, he raises an insightful question: "How does the Law's condemnation of *Jews* stop 'every mouth' and hold 'all the world . . . liable to God?'" He goes on to question, "How does the Law's indictment of *Jews* stop the mouth of *Gentiles* also and hold Jews and Gentiles, together, liable before God?"[73]

Is this a legitimate question? Does Paul really think the law speaks only to Jews in this text, and does he expect someone to understand the inner

---

71. Seifrid renders ὑπόδικος as "guilty." See Seifrid, "Romans," 618; Seifrid, "Unrighteous by Faith," 140; especially, Seifrid, *Christ, Our Righteousness*, 61. He refers to Philo, *Spec. Leg.* 2:249 and Josephus, *Vita* 74 to show that "the sense of 'guilt' or 'liability to judgment' is normally attached to this word." In addition, he points out that in Rom 3:19 "the word *hypodikos* is coupled with the clause, 'that every mouth might be closed', an expression which is regularly used in the Scriptures to describe the silencing of the wicked and guilty (Pss 63:11; 107:42; Job 5:16)."

72. Caneday, "'They Exchanged the Glory of God for the Likeness of an Image,'" 34.

73. Caneday, "'They Exchanged the Glory of God for the Likeness of an Image,'" 34. Italics mine.

logic of the text by asking, "How does the law, speaking to *Jews*, stop every mouth?"[74] In the following, this book will examine the view that only Jews are in the law in Rom 3:19 and will try to consider another possibility with the question "Does not this text indicate that Paul places gentiles along with Jews in the sphere of the law to stop their mouths?" The tentative position of this book is that Rom 3:19 indicates that Paul puts gentiles along with Jews in the sphere of the law, and the law stops their mouths and keeps them under God's judgment along with Jews.

The Position that Only Jews Are in the Law and Gentiles' Mouths Are Stopped by Jews' Hearing the Law

Scholars who believe that Paul places only Jews in the law have provided several suggestions to explain the inner logic of Rom 3:19. The first to be considered is the *a fortiori* view.

The a Fortiori View

This view is the most popular one among scholars who believe Paul places only Jews in the law and Jews' hearing the law stops gentiles' mouths. The most prominent supporters of this view include Barrett, Cranfield, Moo, and Schreiner.[75] Moo conjectures that Paul probably uses "an implicit 'from the greater to the lesser' argument," noting that "if Jews, God's chosen people, cannot be excluded from the scope of sin's tyranny, then it surely follows that Gentiles, who have no claim on God's favor, are also guilty."[76] Schreiner similarly uses the *a fortiori* argument, but he explains this verse in

74. Supporters of the view that the law speaks only to the Jews include Barrett, *Commentary on the Epistle to the Romans*, 70; Cranfield, *Romans 1–8*, 196; Käsemann, *Commentary on Romans*, 87; Dunn, *Romans 1–8*, 152; Morris, *Epistle to the Romans*, 170; Davies, *Faith and Obedience in Romans*, 102; Fitzmyer, *Romans*, 336; Moo, *Epistle to the Romans*, 205–206; Byrne, *Romans*, 117; Schreiner, *Romans*, 168; Jewett, *Romans*, 264; Caneday, "'They Exchanged the Glory of God for the Likeness of an Image,'" 34–45; Matera, *Romans*, 85; Hultgren, *Paul's Letter to the Romans*, 145; Kruse, *Paul's Letter to the Romans*, 170; Rosner, *Paul and the Law*, 52; Thielman, *Romans*, 188; Sherwood, *Romans*, 226; Peterson, *Romans*, 179.

75. Barrett, *Commentary on the Epistle to the Romans*, 70; Cranfield, *Critical and Exegetical Commentary on the Epistle to the Romans*, 196; Moo, *Epistle to the Romans*, 206; Schreiner, *Romans*, 168; Caneday also points out these scholars as representative supporters of this view. Caneday, "'They Exchanged the Glory of God for the Likeness of an Image,'" 34. Other scholars supporting this view include Mounce, *Romans*, 110n181.

76. Moo, *Epistle to the Romans*, 206

terms of Jews' and gentiles' ability to keep the law, saying, "If the Jews, who had the privilege of being God's covenantal and elect people, could not keep the law, then it follows that no one, including the Gentiles, can."[77]

These scholars' position is basically correct in that, if God's chosen people are in the scope of sin's tyranny and could not keep the law, gentiles are less likely to be successful in keeping the law and escaping from sin's tyranny. However, the difficulty with this position is that Rom 3:19 does not indicate that Paul resorts to an *a fortiori* argument to prove gentiles being under God's judgment with mouths stopped. This position seems to press the text too hard to conform to scholars' theological presuppositions without doing proper justice to the text. Neither Rom 3:19, nor the immediate context, nor Paul's entire argument in Rom 1:18—3:18, signifies that Paul employs an *a fortiori* argument for gentiles' ungodliness and being under God's judgment with their mouths closed. Rather than using an *a fortiori* argument, Paul seems to point out gentiles' own knowledge of God and his will, which is manifested by natural revelation, to demonstrate their being under the obligation to honor God by their obedient life. Further, in Rom 2:14–16, Paul places gentiles in the sphere of the Mosaic law, although they apparently did not receive the Mosaic law on Mount Sinai. Regarding this passage, Schreiner understands Paul to be arguing that gentiles possess the law, at least the moral norms of the Mosaic law.[78]

Even further, if anyone seeks to find Paul's *a fortiori* argument in Rom 1:18—3:20, a quite opposite direction of argument is found between Jews and gentiles. Paul makes use of gentiles, who are not the chosen people, to have Jews' mouths stopped (2:1) and to hold Jews under the judgment of God (2:3). Paul's *a fortiori* argument between Jews and gentiles can be explained as follows: "If gentiles, who do not have the written law of Moses, know God and his will, and thereby do the things of the law by nature and are under God's judgment, how much more Jews, who have the Mosaic law and boastfully teach it, are required to do it and consequently will be more severely judged for their failure to do it."

Although the *a fortiori* view rightly portrays the gentiles' less favorable position in relation to the Jews in terms of the covenantal relationship with God, Paul is probably not arguing in Rom 3:19 that gentiles are without excuse and under God's judgment because of their being outside of the covenant and without the written law of Moses. The suggested *a fortiori* view seems not to fit with Paul's overall argument in Rom 1:18—3:18. Romans 3:19 does not indicate that Paul uses an *a fortiori* argument.

77. Schreiner, *Romans*, 168. Schreiner, *Romans*, 2nd ed., 175.

78. Schreiner, *Romans*, 121–25.

The Representative View

Caneday has suggested this view. He believes that Israel is employed as the representative for "humanity's corruption and plight" in Rom 3:19.[79] He states that "As Adam, so also Israel served as a representative type for all humanity. It is for this reason, then, that Paul says 'that whatever the Law says it says to those in the Law's jurisdiction, in order that every mouth may be stopped and all the world may be liable to God.'"[80]

Caneday relies on Rom 1:21–25 to support his view, in which he finds echoes of Adam and Israel in Jer 2:11 and Ps 106:20. According to Caneday, Paul's "allusion in 1:23 to Israel's idolatry grounds his presentation of Israel as representative of 'the whole world' as he closes his indictment of humanity in 3:19."[81] Therefore he explains his case as follows:

> When Israel exchanged the glory of God for the image of a bull that eats grass, Israel acted out under the Law's jurisdiction what the Gentiles did while not possessing the Law. So, when Israel exchanged the glory of God for the image of the likeness of a creature, privileged Israel reenacted Adam's fall and showed that they were idolaters just like the Gentiles.

It may be agreed that Israel has representative or typological roles in Paul's theology. Käsemann states that "the cosmos is represented in exemplary fashion by the Jew" and "Paul's concept of the law . . . presupposes . . . the Jew as typical representative of human piety directed to performance."[82] Nevertheless, it is doubtful that Paul considers Israel's representative role for gentiles in Rom 3:19. First of all, many scholars insist that in Romans chapter 1, Paul does not fault Israel for their idolatry. Moo claims that "Paul is not describing either the fall of Israel or the fall of humankind in Adam" in Rom 1:23.[83] If Paul does not indict Israel in Romans chapter 1, Israel's representative role for gentiles cannot be ascertained in both Romans chapter 1 and Rom 3:19. Paul is not likely to indict gentiles by way of Israel in Rom 1.

Romans 1:21–25 belongs to the larger context of Rom 1:18–32, in which Paul proves gentiles' sinfulness. Paul uses natural revelation and the natural law concept (cf. 1:19–20, 26–7) to prove gentiles' sinfulness. It seems, therefore, that Paul does not indict gentiles by means of the representative Israel in Rom 1:18–32. He rather directly puts gentiles under the

---

79. Caneday, "'They Exchanged the Glory of God for the Likeness of an Image,'" 35.

80. Caneday, "'They Exchanged the Glory of God for the Likeness of an Image,'" 35.

81. Caneday, "'They Exchanged the Glory of God for the Likeness of an Image,'" 36.

82. Käsemann, *Commentary on Romans*, 87–88.

83. Moo, *Epistle to the Romans*, 109.

sphere of the law in order to stop their mouths from articulating an excuse (1:20). Israel's representative role for gentiles has not developed, at least in the first three chapters of Romans. The suggested representative view does not seem to explain the inner logic of Rom 3:19 properly.

The "Test Case" View

Still other possibilities have been introduced to explain the inner logic of Rom 3:19 by those who believe that only Jews are in the law in Rom 3:19. Everett F. Harrison notes two possibilities.[84] The first is a "test case" view. According to this view, Jews are "regarded as a test case for all peoples. If given the same privileges enjoyed by Israel, the rest would likewise have failed." The test case view is somewhat similar to Caneday's representative view but less probable in terms of the textual support for it. Although it is true that gentiles are no different from Jews in their human nature and therefore they would also have failed with the same privileges given to Jews, it is doubtful that Paul is indeed mentioning here Jews' failure as a test case. Romans 3:19 does not imply that Paul considers Jews to be a test case for gentiles. Neither does Rom 1:18—3:18 indicate that Paul uses Jews as a test case for gentiles' possible failure to keep the law.

The "Needless-to-Say" View

The second possibility, which Harrison notes and prefers, is that "the failure of the non-Jews is so patent that it is not a debatable subject; it can be taken for granted as already established (1:18–32). Once it has been determined that the record of the Jew is no better, then judgment is seen as universally warranted."

This view is somewhat similar to the *a fortiori* view. The difference is found, however, in its emphasis on the distinctiveness of gentiles' sinfulness to the extent that "it is not a debatable subject." According to this view, gentiles' failure is so obvious and taken for granted that the law's speaking to Jews is sufficient to point out all peoples being held accountable to God with mouths closed. If Paul's Jewish dialogue partner is taken into consideration, this interpretation may appear attractive. The Jewish dialogue partner may consider Jews to be justified by their being in the covenantal relationship with God and by possessing the Mosaic law. He may then regard gentiles to be obvious sinners due to their being gentiles by birthright. However, Paul is

84. Harrison, *Romans*, 39–40.

not likely to agree with him. Neither is he likely to conclude his entire argument based on his Jewish interlocutor's falsified understanding. Paul does not argue that if Jews, who have the Mosaic law, fail to keep it, gentiles, who do not have the law, should be taken for granted to be silenced because of their less privileged status and obvious sinfulness originating from their being gentile sinners. Paul has been consistent in arguing that neither gentiles nor Jews are treated differently before God based on their having or not-having the written law of Moses. For Paul, it is not the possessors of but the doers of the law who will be justified before God (2:13). In Paul's argument in Romans chapters 1 and 2, both Jews and gentiles have heard the voice of the law and are thereby at risk of being silenced and under God's judgment unless they obey it.

As seen above, many scholars believe that Paul places only Jews in the law in Rom 3:19 and have been trying to explain the inner logic of Rom 3:19 with several suggestions such as the *a fortiori* view, the representative view, the test case view, and the needless-to-say view. However, their suggestions do not seem to be satisfactory in terms of Paul's overall argument in Rom 1:18—3:18 and the evidence of Rom 3:19. Therefore, we need to consider an alternative suggestion in order to understand the inner logic of this text.

The Position That Gentiles Are in the Sphere of the Law in Rom 3:19

Those who believe that Paul places only Jews in the law in Rom 3:19 raise the following question to explain the inner logic of the text: "How does the Law's condemnation of *Jews* stop 'every mouth' and hold 'all the world . . . liable to God'?" Likewise, we can start our discussion about an alternative suggestion with this question: "Does not this text indicate that Paul places gentiles along with Jews in the sphere of the law to stop every mouth?" If we can agree that Paul indicates gentiles being in the law in Rom 3:19, the inner logic of the text can be better understood.

Proponents of the View that Gentiles are in the Law in Rom 3:19

John Murray is probably the most well known proponent of the view that Paul includes gentiles in the law in Rom 3:19.[85] Almost all scholars who argue that gentiles are excluded from the sphere of the law in this text refer to Murray and most of them refer only to Murray to explain away

85. For his view, see Murray, *Epistle to the Romans*, 1:105–107.

the view that gentiles are included in the law. For instance, Cranfield, Moo, Jewett, and Rosner refer only to Murray.[86] This phenomenon implies that this alternative view is a relatively minority one and has not been seriously considered among scholars. N. T. Wright's 2002 commentary, Richard N. Longenecker's 2016 commentary, and Frank Thielman's 2018 commentary do not mention this alternative view. Schreiner, who refers only to Murray in his 1998 Romans commentary, adds L. E. Keck in his 2018 commentary.[87]

Even further, Murray's view was misunderstood by Cranfield. Referring to Murray unfavorably by the words "*Pace* Murray," Cranfield states that "the emphatic πᾶν and πᾶς . . . are no reason at all for thinking that by τοῖς ἐν τῷ νόμῳ Paul did not mean the Jews."[88] Murray, however, never states that Paul did not mean the Jews by τοῖς ἐν τῷ νόμῳ ("those who are in the law"). Rather, he questions whether only Jews are meant by τοῖς ἐν τῷ νόμῳ. Other supporters for the view that gentiles also are in the law in Rom 3:19 include Brice L. Martin, Neil Elliott, Peter Stuhlmacher, Richard H. Bell and Herbert Bowsher.[89] In the following we will consider the question, "Does not this text indicate that Paul places gentiles along with Jews in the sphere of the law to stop every mouth?"

"Every Mouth" and "All the World"

Käsemann and Matera insist that "every mouth" and "all the world" refer to Jews.[90] However, Fitzmyer and Longenecker rightly point out that these expressions, "every mouth" and "all the world," are used for all mankind, both Jews and gentiles.[91] The words "every mouth" and "all the world"

86. Cranfield, *Romans 1–8*, 196; Moo, *Epistle to the Romans*, 205; Jewett, *Romans*, 264; Rosner, *Paul and the Law*, 53.

87. Wright, *Letter to the Romans*; Longenecker, *Epistle to the Romans*; Thielman, *Romans*; Schreiner, *Romans*, 2nd ed., 175; Keck, *Romans*, 99.

88. Cranfield, *Romans 1–8*, 196.

89. Martin, *Christ and the Law in Paul*, 103; Elliott, *Rhetoric of Romans*, 142–46; Stuhlmacher, *Paul's Letter to the Romans*, 55; Bell, *No One Seeks for God*, 223; Bowsher, "To Whom Does the Law Speak?," 295–303.

90. Käsemann states that "'world' here is not just defined by the totality of mankind, but concretely by the contrast between Jew and gentile. The 'every' and 'all' have the Jew specifically in mind." Käsemann, *Commentary on Romans*, 87; So also, Matera, *Romans*, 86: "when Paul speaks of 'the whole world' here, he appears to be referring to the Jewish world."

91. Fitzmyer, *Romans*, 337; Longenecker, *The Epistle to the Romans*, 359: "So 'the whole world,' both Gentiles *and* Jews, are 'under sin' and 'legally accountable' before God." The majority of scholars agree on this: Dunn, *Romans 1–8*, 152; Morris, *Epistle to the Romans*, 170–71; Black, *Romans*, 56; Moo, *Epistle to the Romans*, 205; Schreiner,

in Rom 3:19 imply that Paul might have thought all human beings including gentiles to be in the law. Although many scholars try to explain why the law's condemnation of *Jews* stops every mouth and puts all the world under God's judgment, their efforts seem not to be successful. They try to interpret this text with the presupposition that Paul could not have said gentiles are in the law because they did not receive the Mosaic law. However, this text provides a clue that he might have thought all human beings are in the law. By mentioning "every mouth" and "all the world" right after referring to those who are in the law, Paul seems to reveal his understanding of the relationship between the law and all human beings, that is, all human beings are in the sphere of the law. Murray also finds the words "every mouth" and "the whole world" as indicating that Paul places gentiles in the law.[92]

Romans 3:9–18

The immediate context, that is Rom 3:9–18, supports the view that Paul includes gentiles in the law in Rom 3:19. Paul claims in 3:9 that "all people, both Jews and Greeks, are under sin" (Ἰουδαίους τε καὶ Ἕλληνας πάντας ὑφ' ἁμαρτίαν εἶναι). Then, in 3:10–18 he provides the proof for his assertion that all human beings are sinners. Paul's catena in these verses, as Neil Elliott observes, "refers *not only* to the Jews."[93] Although Elliott is not likely correct in his argument that Jews are not Paul's target of critique in this passage,[94] he is correct at least in his assertion that the catena refers to both Jews and gentiles. In 3:19, Paul applies his catena to "those who are in the law" and then connects "those who are in the law" to "every mouth" and "all the world." Paul's words "those who are in the law" are sandwiched between Paul's catena, which refers to all human beings, and his mention of "every mouth" and "all the world." Since Paul's catena in 3:10–18 refers to Jews and gentiles, Paul seems to refer to Jews and gentiles as well by the expression "those who are in the law," to which the catena is directed.

Scholars seem to reject the view that gentiles are included in "those who are in the law" because the law in 3:19 can be identified with the catena in 3:10–18. For instance, Moo notes that "this view has against it the close identification of *nomos* with the written Scripture in this context (cf. vv.

Romans, 168–69; Jewett, *Romans*, 264; Caneday, "'They Exchanged the Glory of God for the Likeness of an Image,'" 34; Middendorf, *Romans 1–8*, 255.

92. Murray, *Epistle to the Romans*, 106.

93. Elliott, *Rhetoric of Romans*, 142.

94. Elliott, *Rhetoric of Romans*, 141–46.

10–11)."[95] It has been widely agreed among scholars that the *nomos* in the words "whatever *the law* (νόμος) says" refers to the catena in the previous verses.[96] Paul's catena comes from Psalms and Isaiah rather than the Pentateuch. However, the fact that Paul uses the word *nomos* in a wider concept comprising not only the Mosaic law but the Old Testament does not warrant that Paul does not include gentiles in the law in Rom 3:19.[97] By using *nomos*, which refers to the Old Testament, Paul may indicate that gentiles are in the sphere of the Old Testament as well as the Mosaic law.[98] Paul's applying the Old Testament to gentiles is not uncommon in his letters. For instance, he puts gentiles under the authority of the Old Testament in Rom 15:4. Having cited Ps 69:9 (68:10 LXX) in Rom 15:3, Paul states in Rom 15:4 that the Old Testament was written for Jews' and gentiles' instruction:[99]

> For whatever was written in earlier times was written for our instruction, that through perseverance and encouragement of the Scriptures we might have hope.[100] (NASB)

In the context of Romans chapters 14 and 15, Paul considers Ps 69:9 to be speaking particularly to gentile believers in Rome. Paul hears the Old Testament speaking to gentile believers, that is the "strong," to receive their "weak" Jewish Christians.[101] According to Seifrid, "even the words of the Davidic psalm speak to believers now, including *Gentile readers*."[102] In Paul's mind, Jewish Scriptures were not written only for Jews. They were written for both Jews and gentiles and continue to speak to all human beings. The idea that only Jews are "in the law" because Paul uses the word *nomos* with the sense of the Old Testament fails to grasp Paul's understanding of the relationship between the Old Testament and gentiles. Nor is it compatible

95. Moo, *Epistle to the Romans*, 205.

96. Barrett, *Commentary on the Epistle to the Romans*, 70; Cranfield, *Romans 1–8*, 195.

97. Wright understands that the Torah here was "taken as the whole of the Jewish scripture, not mearly as the first five books." Wright, *Letter to the Romans*, 458.

98. Paul's use of *nomos* as a reference to the Old Testament is also observed in 1 Cor 14:21.

99. Schreiner comments regarding Rom 15:4 that "the OT Scriptures were written 'for our instruction,' that is, for both Jews and Gentiles." Schreiner, *Romans*, 748.

100. Considering the context, the "we" in Rom 15:4 are the "we who are strong" in 15:1. Those whom Paul refers to as the strong are the predominant gentile Christians in Rome, who can eat any meat, do not regard a specific day as more sacred, and are not bound by the Old Testament purity laws. Therefore, the "we" in 15:4 can be understood as Paul and the predominant gentile Christians in Rome.

101. Seifrid, "Romans," 686.

102. Seifrid, "Romans," 687. Italics added.

with Paul's frequent authoritative citation of the Old Testament for gentiles.[103] Romans 3:19 is likely to reveal Paul's theology that both Jews and gentiles are under the law, which can refer to the Mosaic law and the Old Testament, and consequently they are under its condemnation.

Romans 1:18—3:8

The wider context, Rom 1:18—3:8, supports the view that Paul might include gentiles in the law in Rom 3:19. As scholars have observed, Rom 3:19-20 function as a conclusion for Rom 1:18—3:18.[104] Therefore, Paul's earlier argument in Rom 1:18—3:8 may help us to understand his concluding remarks in Rom 3:19. Although Stuhlmacher does not explain 1:18—3:8 in detail in his comments on 3:19, he aptly refers to that part for the view that Paul includes gentiles in the law in 3:19. Regarding "those who are in the law," he states, "According to 2:17-24 this is first of all the Jews. But according to 1:20ff., 32; 2:14ff., 26 this also includes the Greek Gentiles."[105]

Paul argues in Rom 1:18—3:8 that all people, Jews and gentiles, are sinners before God and that they are under his wrath. In Romans chapter 1, Paul indicts gentiles for their sinfulness by the natural law concept. They know God and his will by natural revelation. They know "the ordinance of God" (1:32), which proclaims the death penalty to sinners. Thielman contends that "the ordinance of God" in Rom 1:32 refers to the Mosaic law and Schreiner comments that "Gentiles, without specifically having the Mosaic law, are aware of the moral requirements contained in that law."[106] Paul seems to place gentiles in the sphere of the Mosaic law by means of natural law and revelation and holds them under the judgment of the Mosaic law.

In chapter 2, Paul deals with Jews' sinfulness. God provided the law to Jews so that they may keep them and be righteous before God. However, they failed to obey it and consequently "will be judged by the law" (Rom 2:12). Paul contends that merely possessing the Mosaic law does not avail for Jews' righteousness, because the doers of the law will be justified (Rom 2:13). Against those Jews who consider themselves to be righteous before

103. Schreiner points out that Paul cites "the Old Testament as authoritative for Gentile churches." Schreiner, *Law and Its Fulfillment*, 38.

104. Schreiner, *Romans*, 161, 168 and 172.

105. Stuhlmacher, *Paul's Letter to the Romans*, 55; Rather cautiously, Middendorf puts, "As a result and *to the extent* that his common 'work of the Law' is 'written' (γραπτὸν, 2:15), Gentiles too are 'within the Law' (ἐν τῷ νόμῳ, 3:19)." Middendorf, *Romans 1–8*, 254. emphasis original.

106. Thielman, *Paul and the Law*, 169. Schreiner, *Romans*, 99.

God on the ground that they possess the Mosaic law, Paul demonstrates that gentiles also have the Mosaic law and do it occasionally (Rom 2:14–16).

Although gentiles do not have the written law of Moses, in Paul's view they actually have the law as well. They have the Mosaic law written in their hearts. They know God's will and sometimes follow or go against it in their behavior (Rom 1:16, 27; 2:14). Their conscience witnesses their having the law, and this law will be used as a standard for gentiles' judgment (2:15, 16). Paul's most powerful assertion regarding gentiles having the law is found in his proclamation that "they are the law to themselves" (2:14). Paul places gentiles in the law in his argument against Jews' belief that possessing the Mosaic law is "a sign of salvation."[107]

By the assertion that both Jews and gentiles are in the law, Paul establishes two consequences: (1) Gentiles are without excuse (ἀναπολογήτους, 1:20) and under the judgment of God (2:16, cf.1:32) when they worship idols and act against God's will (1:18–32). They have heard God's law. Only doers will be justified. (2) Jews are without excuse (ἀναπολόγητος, 2:1) and under the judgment of God (2:2, 3). Although they condemn gentiles and boast of possessing the law, if they do not keep the law, they are equally under the wrath of God as gentiles. God provides a fair standard to both Jews and gentiles, that is "works of the law." Only doers will be justified.

After this argument for all people being sinners in the light of God's law, either the written or the unwritten law of Moses, Paul comes to a conclusion in Rom 3:19. In these concluding remarks, Paul recapitulates two consequences for every sinner: (1) Every mouth is stopped (cf. without excuse [1:20, 2:1]); (2) All the world is held guilty before God (cf. judgment of God [1:32; 2:2, 3, 15]). These two consequences are the same as Jews and gentiles face in Romans chapters 1 and 2 by their being in the law.

In Rom 3:19, on what ground does Paul conclude that all people, Jews and gentiles, are without excuse (i.e., closed mouth) and under the judgment of God (i.e., being held guilty before God)? It is the law, which speaks to *those who are in the law* (ἐν τῷ νόμῳ). Then, to whom does the law speak? Does Paul indicate that the law speaks only to Jews here? Does he indeed expect readers of this letter to speculate on the relationship between the law's speaking to Jews and all human beings' responsibility here? Or otherwise, as this book presumes, does he want to reemphasize the fact that Jews and gentiles have heard the law and all of them are without excuse and under God's judgment according to the law? Considering its concluding aspect

---

107. Regarding Rom 2:14–15, Schreiner states that "what Paul wants to prove here is that the Jews should not consider possessing the Mosaic law as a sign of salvation because even the Gentiles who do not have the Mosaic law have heard the law." Schreiner, "Did Paul Believe in Justification by Works?" 145.

and Paul's argument in the preceding chapters, Rom 3:19 seems to indicate that Paul places gentiles along with Jews in the sphere of the law to stop all their mouths and put them under God's fair judgment, which will be applied to them according to their works of the law.

"Now We Know That"—Hellenistic Judaism's Understanding of the Law's Relation to Gentiles

Paul begins Rom 3:19 by stating, *"Now we know that* whatever the law says, it speaks to those who are in the law" (ἐν τῷ νόμῳ). Do Hellenistic Jews ("we know") understand that gentiles are in the law and hear the law speaking to them? As the second chapter of this book has demonstrated, there are evidences that Hellenistic Jews thought that gentiles are in the law and its judgment by being aware of it. The Mosaic law's universality is particularly emphasized in the context of God's judgment over the world in Hellenistic Judaism. Fourth Ezra 7:37, 72, 13:37–38 indicates that gentiles will be judged by the law because they despised God's commandments. Fourth Ezra 7:73 contends that gentiles will be without excuse before the judgment seat of God due to their knowledge of the law. Second Baruch 15:5–6 and 48:39–40 note that gentiles will understand God's judgment because they have received the law and been instructed with understanding. They consequently know when they act unrighteously.

In Hellenistic Judaism, the Mosaic law is presented as a universal norm speaking to gentiles as well as to Jews to place all human beings under the sphere of the Mosaic law. The concept of natural law is employed to claim the Mosaic law's universal validity. For Ben Sira, the Mosaic law is an embodiment of natural law, which existed as wisdom all over the world. Sirach 44:20 remarks that even Abraham had observed the Mosaic law even before it was given to Israel. Philo regards the Mosaic law as a representation of nature's purpose and will. Mosaic law is available to all who use reason, since it is a copy of the natural law.

In conclusion, many scholars believe that Paul includes only Jews in the law in Rom 3:19. Thus, they have been facing the question, "How does the law's speaking to *Jews* stop every mouth and hold all the world accountable to God?" Although they provide several suggestions to answer this question, such as the *a fortiori* view, the representative view, the test case view and the needless-to-say view, their solutions are not successful in explaining the inner logic of the text.

The inner logic of this verse seems to be better understood when we consider the possibility that Paul might have placed gentiles along with Jews in the law in this verse. This interpretation is supported by (1) the words "every mouth" and "all the world" in 3:9, (2) Paul's argument in Rom 3:9–18, (3) his argument in Rom 1:18—3:8, and (4) Hellenistic Judaism's putting gentiles within the sphere of the law. In Rom 3:19 Paul concludes his argument that all human beings are under the wrath of God by claiming that all people, Jews and gentiles, are in sphere of the law. All of them have heard the law speaking to them. Therefore, they are without excuse for their ungodliness. All of them are subject to God's judgment, which will be performed according to the law.

ROMANS 3:20: WHOM DOES PAUL ADDRESS?

Understanding the fact that Paul places gentiles in the law plays an important role in one's understanding of what Paul means in Rom 3:20. In Rom 3:20, Paul proclaims that "by the works of the law no flesh will be justified in his sight." In this proclamation, whom does Paul have in mind? Does he address Rom 3:20 only to Jews, thinking that only Jews are in the law and practice "works of the law"? Does Paul declare to Jews that no Jews will be justified by their particular works of the law? Or otherwise does he proclaim generally to all human beings that no one of them will be justified by works of the law? Many scholars, mostly those supporting New Perspective, argue that Paul is referring to Jews and their failure to be justified by works of the law here. In the following, we will deal with the question, "To whom does Paul address Rom 3:20?"

To Jews Regarding Their Works of the Law

There are some scholars who argue that Rom 3:20 is addressed to the Jews regarding their failure of being justified by their works of the law. James D. G. Dunn, one of the most significant proponents of "New Perspective on Paul," holds this view. He insists that Rom 3:20 is addressed "particularly to Jews":

> Clearest and most significant of all is the way in which Paul introduces 3.20. This summary indictment (in terms of 'works of the law') is addressed *particularly to Jews*: 'we know that whatever the law says it says to those within the law, in order that every mouth might be stopped . . .' (3:19).[108]

108. Dunn, "Yet Once More—'Works of the Law,'" 105 [= Dunn, "Yet Once More—'Works of the Law,'" in *The New Perspective on Paul*, 218]. Dunn's emphasis.

Dunn's understanding of Rom 3:20 is based on his interpretation of Rom 3:19. Thinking that Paul refers to Jews in Rom 3:19 in terms of law's speaking to those "within the law," Dunn maintains that Rom 3:20, the very next verse, is also addressed *"particularly to Jews."*[109] However, this approach to Rom 3:20 based on Rom 3:19 cannot be warranted since Rom 3:19 proves that Paul places gentiles along with Jews "within the law" as we explored above.

Dunn continues to argue that Paul has the Jews in mind in his referring to the law in Rom 3:20:

> His target was rather the devout Jew in his presupposition that as a member of the covenant people he could expect God's righteousness to be put forth because he was "within the law."[110]

> When Paul speaks of 'justification by works of the law' *he can have only one people in mind*—Israel, the Jews in general. The only law in view is the Jewish law. Only the Jews (in general) cherished this law; only they thought in terms of 'works of the law' and of 'justification' in terms of the law. When, therefore, Paul speaks of 'no flesh' as being justified by works of the law, he clearly means to ensure that his fellow Jews recognize that they *specifically* are *not* exempt. The emphasis on 'flesh' is apposite, since it should remind the 'Jew' of his particular trust in the flesh (2.28–29; cf. Phil. 3.4).[111]

According to Dunn, Paul's target in Rom 3:20 is devout Jews regarding *their* "works of the law." Therefore, "works of the law" in Rom 3:20 is "Jewish particular."[112] Dunn emphasizes that Paul *"can have only one people in mind"* when he maintains the impossibility of justification by works of the law. The reason for his applying this verse to Jews can be found in his statement that "the only law in view is the Jewish law. Only the Jews (in general) cherished this law." Since gentiles are not "within the law," in Dunn's view, "works of the law" are not the gentiles' issue. For him, the inability of "works of the law" to provide righteousness is a Jewish sociological problem with

---

109. Commenting on Rom 3:19, Dunn insists that "the Jews are defined as 'those within the law.'" In this verse, Dunn says, "the character and function of the law as marking the boundary between Jews and Gentiles comes to expression." Dunn, *Romans, 1–8*, 152.

110. Dunn, *Romans, 1–8*, 155.

111. Dunn, "Yet Once More—'Works of the Law,'" 105. The italics are original. Also Dunn, *Theology of Paul the Apostle*, 354–55.

112. Dunn, *Romans 1–8*, 153.

the law, which functions as a boundary marker between Jews and gentiles.[113] Regarding the meaning of "works of the law," Dunn tries, in responding to his critics,[114] to make clear that he does not restrict "works of the law" to such particular requirements of the law as circumcision, keeping food laws, and the observance of the Sabbath.[115] He explicitly affirms that "'works of the law' refers to what the law requires, the conduct prescribed by the Torah; whatever the law requires to be done can be described as 'doing' the law, as a work of the law."[116] However, it can be observed that Dunn virtually restricts "works of the law" to circumcision and food laws in his argument, because he claims that these issues are the very particular points Paul deals with in his reference to "works of the law," and Dunn adheres to this concept in his argument about the "works of the law."[117] He seems to try to rebut his critics' responses by saying that "works of the law" means the whole law but Paul specifically has in mind the identity markers such as circumcision, food laws and the Sabbath with this term. Nevertheless, there is a more serious problem remaining. It is his restricting "works of the law" to the Jews. According to Dunn, the failure of "works of the law" as a means of justification is particularly a Jewish failure. For Dunn, Paul reminds the Jews of their failure to be justified by their boundary markers such as circumcision, food laws, and the Sabbath observance. Is this a legitimate understanding of Paul in this verse? Does not Paul place gentiles as well as Jews in the law and proclaim that all human beings will fail to be justified by their works of the law here?

N. T. Wright also believes that Paul is referring to Jews in Rom 3:20. He states, "We remind ourselves again that he is not speaking of Gentiles here, but of Jews."[118] He understands that Paul refers by "works of the law" to the Jewish performance of the law rather than human beings' observance of the law. For Wright, "works of the law" are the sign of the "membership in Israel, God's covenant people."[119] Highlighted elements as "works of the law" in Romans and Galatians are the ethnic demarcation such as

---

113. Dunn, *Romans 1–8*, 153–55. See also Longenecker, *Eschatology and the Covenant*, 200–202.

114. Including Cranfield who rejects Dunn's restricted sense of ἔργα νόμου. See Cranfield, "'Works of the Law' in the Epistle to the Romans," 89–101.

115. Dunn, "New Perspective on Paul: Whence, What and Whither?," in *New Perspective on Paul*, 23–28; Dunn, "Yet Once More—'Works of the Law,'" 100–102.

116. Dunn, "New Perspective on Paul: Whence, What and Whither?," 23–24.

117. Dunn, "Yet Once More—'Works of the Law,'" 100–102.

118. Wright, *Letter to the Romans*, 459.

119. Wright, *Letter to the Romans*, 460.

circumcision, the Sabbath, and the food laws.[120] What, then, does Paul really say in Rom 3:20 when he claims that by works of the law *no flesh* will be justified? Wright argues, "Paul's fundamental meaning is that *no Jew* can use possession of the Torah, and performance of its key symbolic 'works' of ethnic demarcation, as demonstration in the present time that they belong to the eschatological people of God, the people who will inherit the age to come."[121] Just as Dunn, Wright understands Rom 3:20 to be addressed to the Jews regarding their works of the law. For him, rejecting the law as the means of justification is an ethnic issue rather than an ethical issue relevant to all human beings under the law.

Although Dunn and Wright endeavor to interpret Rom 3:20 with the view that Paul addresses the Jews regarding their failure to gain favor before God by their covenantal privilege, Rom 3:20 as well as the immediate context does not support their interpretation. It is obvious that Paul proclaims to all human beings their failure to be justified by works of the law by placing all human beings under the light of the law.

To All Human Beings, Jews, and Gentiles, Regarding Their Works of the Law

Romans 3:20 and its context provide evidence that Paul addresses Rom 3:20 to all human beings, that is Jews and gentiles. Paul uses "works of the law" as what all human beings do rather than what only Jews do. Paul places gentiles as well as Jews in the law in his reasoning for condemnation and salvation of human beings. Therefore, those who do "works of the law" include gentiles as well as Jews. The following will show this aspect.

The Flow of Argument from Rom 3:19–20

In Rom 3:19, Paul places gentiles in the sphere of the law along with Jews. Gentiles hear the law speaking to them, and consequently all mouths—Jews and gentiles—become closed and the whole world is held guilty before God. The reason why all mouths and all the world—again Jews and gentiles— are in this state is articulated in Rom 3:20: "because (διότι) by the works of the Law no flesh will be justified (οὐ δικαιωθήσεται πᾶσα σάρξ) in His sight"(NASB).

120. Wright, *Letter to the Romans*, 461.

121. Wright, *Letter to the Romans*, 463–64. Italics added.

One element that is not seriously considered by the supporters of the New Perspective is the conjunction διότι in 3:20. Paul's argument in Rom 3:19 is continued in Rom 3:20 by διότι. As Schreiner rightly observes, Paul provides in 3:20 the reason for his contention in 3:19—being silenced and held guilty before God—by using διότι.[122] Robert Jewett also states, διότι in 3:20 "draws the entire final sentence into relationship to the earlier discourse of the pericope, providing the underlying reason for the divine action of silencing human evasions and holding all to be accountable."[123] If "every mouth (πᾶν στόμα)" and "all the world (πᾶς ὁ κόσμος)" denote all human beings, and if Rom 3:20 explains why they are in the state of being silenced and guilty before God by using διότι, it is most reasonable to think that Paul applies Rom 3:20 to all human beings, not just Jews. Indeed, there is no reason to restrict Rom 3:20 to the Jews, especially in this context. Paul provides the reason why all human beings are sinners before God in this verse. "Works of the law" cannot make all humans beings—"every mouth" and "all the world"—stand righteous before God. The universal sinfulness of human beings is expressed by Paul in his directly relating all human beings to their "works of the law." There is no evidence that Paul indirectly speaks of the universal sinfulness by pointing out Jews' sinfulness in Rom 3:20, since Rom 3:20 is stated regarding "all mouths" and "all the world." In this context, it is evident that "works of the law" is used here in Rom 3:20 as something on which all human beings might depend for justification but fail to obtain.

However, Dunn understands that Paul addresses Rom 3:20 to Jews who are "within the law," thinking that Paul "*can have only one people in mind*" in his reference to "justification by works of the law."[124] He further argues, regarding "works of the law," that "here too 'works of the law' (3:20) have in view the obligations which the Torah of Israel laid upon *Israel*."[125] Of course, "works of the law" can be applied to Israel, the Torah-given people, since Paul relates it to all human beings. Nevertheless, it is important to understand that "works of the law" cannot be restricted to Israel in Rom 3:20. The defection of "works of the law" as the means of justification is applied to all human beings. Paul places gentiles as well as Jews within the law and relates all of them to "works of the law," demonstrating that they cannot be justified by "works of the law."

---

122. Schreiner, *Romans*, 169. So also Murray, *Epistle to the Romans*, 1:107.

123. Jewett, *Romans*, 265.

124. Dunn, "Yet Once More—'Works of the Law,'" 105. The italics are original.

125. Dunn, "Whatever Happened to 'Works of the Law'?," in *New Perspective on Paul*, 383. Italics added.

"No Flesh Will Be Justified in His Sight"

Who are those who cannot be justified by works of the law? Paul uses the words πᾶσα σάρξ to identify them in Rom 3:20: "By the works of the law *no flesh* will be justified in his sight (ἐξ ἔργων νόμου οὐ δικαιωθήσεται πᾶσα σάρξ ἐνώπιον αὐτοῦ)." Does Paul refer to Jews only or all human beings here by πᾶσα σάρξ? Dunn tries to evade the sense of all human beings in πᾶσα σάρξ by arguing that it describes "human finitude, weakness and corruptibility in contrast to God."[126] He even conjectures that Paul might have thought the Jewish particular by σάρξ. According to Dunn, Paul uses "all flesh" to articulate "the fleshly distinctiveness of which the loyal Jew makes boast, particularly his circumcision 'in the flesh.'"[127] For Dunn, therefore, πᾶσα σάρξ has a negative nuance, and a nationalistic or ethnic meaning with relation to Jews.

However, πᾶσα σάρξ can be better understood as referring to human beings. "Flesh" is used in the Old Testament to simply mean human beings.[128] Genesis 6:12 refers to human beings by "flesh" ("God looked on the earth . . . all flesh had corrupted their way upon the earth [κατέφθειρεν πᾶσα σάρξ τὴν ὁδὸν αὐτοῦ ἐπὶ τῆς γῆς]"). Genesis 6:12 LXX employs πᾶσα σάρξ (כָּל־בָּשָׂר , MT) to point out that all human beings were found guilty before the eyes of God which look on the earth ("God looked on the earth."). By πᾶσα σάρξ in Rom 3:20, Paul may allude to Gen 6:12.[129] Employing πᾶσα σάρξ, Paul claims, "no flesh will be justified in his sight." Just like Gen 6:12, Rom 3:20 seems to insist that all human beings ("no flesh/ πᾶσα σάρξ) are found guilty in the sight of God (ἐνώπιον αὐτοῦ).

In addition, it has been suggested by many scholars that Paul alludes to Ps 143:2 (142:2 LXX) by Rom 3:20.[130] Psalm 142:2 LXX and Rom 3:20 share common words and forms:

> Ps 142:2— οὐ δικαιωθήσεται ἐνώπιόν σου πᾶς ζῶν
> ("no one living will be justified in your sight")
> Rom 3:20— οὐ δικαιωθήσεται πᾶσα σάρξ ἐνώπιον αὐτοῦ
> ("no flesh will be justified in his sight")

126. Dunn, *Romans 1–8*, 155.

127. Dunn, *Romans 1–8*, 155.

128. Moo states, "'Flesh' was a common way of referring to human beings in the OT." Moo, *Epistle to the Romans*, 206n54. Käsemann, *Commentary on Romans*, 88.

129. Seifrid notes that Paul alludes to Gen 6:12 with the expression πᾶσα σάρξ, though he does not explain this in detail. Seifrid, "*Romans*," 618.

130. Cranfield, *Romans 1–8*, 198; Dunn, *Romans 1–8*, 152–53; Moo, *Epistle to the Romans*, 206; Wright, *Romans*, 459.

In Rom 3:20, Paul replaces "no one living (οὐ . . . πᾶς ζῶν)" with "no flesh (οὐ . . . πᾶσα σάρξ)." This replacement connotes that Paul uses "no flesh" in the same meaning as "no one living," which refers to all human beings living on earth in Ps 142 LXX.[131] As the Psalmist confesses that all human beings are sinners before God, Paul proclaims in Rom 3:20 that all human beings are sinners before God. In light of this allusion, we can conclude that Paul refers to all human beings, not just Jews, in his contention that *no flesh* will be justified by works of the law.

In 1 Enoch, "flesh" is also used to refer to human beings.[132] Having read the tablet(s) of heaven, Enoch states in 1 Enoch 81:2, "I read that book and all the deeds of humanity and all the children of the flesh upon the earth for all the generations of the world." Here "flesh" simply means human beings as "humanity" does. In this context, the "seven holy ones" say to Enoch similar words to those we find in Rom 3:20, "Make everything known to your son, Methuselah, and show to all your children that *no one of the flesh can be just before the Lord*; for they are merely his own creation" (1 Enoch 81:5). Considering the immediate context, "flesh" in 1 Enoch 81:5 can be understood as referring to human beings. Here "flesh" is depicted as the result of God's creation, seemingly being identified as created human beings. Thus, what Enoch was told is that no one of human beings can be just before God. Because of the similarity in wording between 1 Enoch 81:5 and Rom 3:20, some have suggested that Romans was influenced by Enoch.[133] Whether Paul was actually influenced by Enoch 81:5 is subject to debate. However, it can at least be claimed that Paul uses "flesh" to refer to human beings as we find an example in 1 Enoch 81:5.

"Flesh" is sometimes used as a heavily loaded term in Paul's letters. Because of this, some scholars try to interpret πᾶσα σάρξ in Rom 3:20 as nuanced words denoting "human finitude, weakness and corruptibility."[134] However, this aspect should not be overemphasized in Rom 3:20 in which Paul employs "flesh" simply to refer to human beings. In this regard, Moo's comment is helpful: "'Flesh' was a common way of referring to human beings in the OT; and this makes it very improbable that we should find any

---

131. Frank Thielman understands Ps 143:2 (142:2 LXX) as "a general statement that in God's presence no one can claim to be righteous." Thielman, *Law and the New Testament*, 37.

132. First Enoch is a pseudepigraphon known to be written in the second century BC–the first century AD. This work is composite and originated in Judea. For the introduction of 1 Enoch, see Isaac, "1 (Ethiopic Apocalypse of) Enoch," in *Old Testament Pseudepigrapha*, vol. 1, *Apocalyptic Literature and Testaments*, 5–12.

133. Jewett, *Romans*, 265.

134. Dunn, *Romans 1–8*, 155.

negative nuance in Paul's use of σὰρξ here (contra Dunn)."[135] When Paul proclaims that no flesh will be justified in God's sight by works of the law, he simply points out that no human being, Jew or gentile, can be justified before God by works.

As seen already, Dunn believes that "all flesh" is used to refer to the Jewish particular. "All flesh" includes, according to Dunn, "the fleshly distinctiveness of which the loyal Jew makes boast, particularly his circumcision 'in the flesh.'"[136] Wright also interprets it as "Jewish 'flesh'" and "the 'fleshly' badge of circumcision."[137] Scholars' thus relating "flesh" to circumcision is not persuasive. Paul addresses all human beings in his statement that no flesh will be justified by works of the law, since "πᾶσα σὰρξ" refers to gentiles as well as Jews.

Then, why do some scholars try to restrict the meaning of "all flesh" to the Jews and labor to understand Rom 3:20 as meaning that Jews cannot be justified by works of the Jewish law such as circumcision and keeping the food laws? First, their exegetical conclusion comes from their presupposition about the meaning of "works of the law." "Works of the law" is understood in this verse as referring to Jewish observance of the law as ethnic demarcation in the covenantal relationship with God. In order to support this predetermined interpretation of "works of the law," they seem to distort the meaning of "all flesh" to be "all fleshly Jews" instead of "all human beings." Second, their interpretation of this verse comes from their misunderstanding of Paul's skillful way of presenting his gospel to the Roman congregation: placing gentiles as well as Jews under the law. Since Jews and gentiles are "within the law" in Rom 3:19–20, "works of the law" is what Jews and gentiles do. Interpretation of Rom 3:20 should not begin with the predetermined meaning of "works of the law" without doing proper justice to the context and words such as διότι and "πᾶσα σὰρξ." In Rom 3:20 Paul concludes his claim in 3:9–19 that all human beings are sinners.[138] Thus, Rom 3:20 needs to be understood as Paul's address to all human beings who are in the sphere of the law.

135. Moo, *Epistle to the Romans*, 206n54. Ben Witherington shows a similar view. See Witherington, *Paul's Letter to the Romans*, 96n33.

136. Dunn, *Romans 1–8*, 155.

137. Wright, *Letter to the Romans*, 459.

138. Thielman, *Law and the New Testament*, 37.

No Flesh by "Works of the Law"

Paul proclaims in Rom 3:20 that no one, Jew or gentile, can be justified by "works of the law" before God. Failing to be justified by "works of the law" is, therefore, not only a Jewish issue but also an "all human beings" issue. "Works of the law" cannot be restricted to the Jewish identity markers separating Jews from gentiles, since gentiles also do the things of the law and fail to be justified (cf. Rom 2:14). It is natural, then, to understand "works of the law" as *human beings*, not just Jews, doing *all the requirements* of the law, rather than just a particular demands of the law such as circumcision, keeping purity laws and the observance of the Sabbath.[139] In other words, the meaning of "works of the law" in Rom 3:20 can be understood as human beings keeping the law or "deeds done in obedience to the law of Moses."[140]

Why, then, cannot "works of the law" or law make human beings stand righteous before God? Schreiner's survey of the scholars' solution is useful.[141] Lloyd Gaston, who takes νόμος as a subjective genitive, insists that the works which the law does are evil.[142] Hans Hübner and Günter Klein argue that even the perfect keeper of the law is a sinner because his desire to be saved by obeying the law is idolatry.[143] E. P. Sanders' view is that "works of the law" was excluded by Paul as a way of salvation after he believed in Christ and thought "from solution to plight." Paul reasoned, according to Sanders, that if Christ is the way, the law is not the way for salvation although there is no problem with it.[144] For James Dunn, the problem of "works of the law" is Jewish nationalism, which separates Jews from gentiles based on the Jewish notion of privilege.[145]

Gaston's view can be rejected because the "works" referred to in Romans chapters 3 and 4 mean the "deeds done by humans" rather than the law.[146] As Westerholm points out, "works" in Rom 4:2 means Abraham's

---

139. Scholars who regard "works of the law" as all the law requires or as "general sense" rather than "restricted sense" include Cranfield, "'The Works of the Law' in the Epistle to the Romans," 89–101; Schreiner, *New Testament Theology*, 527.

140. Seifrid, *Christ, Our Righteousness*, 100. So also Moo, "'Law,' 'Works of the Law,' and Legalism in Paul," 96.

141. Schreiner, *Law and Its Fulfillment*, 42–44; Schreiner, *Romans*, 169–72; Schreiner, *New Testament Theology*, 526–27.

142. Gaston, *Paul and the Torah*, 100–107.

143. Hübner, *Law in Paul's Thought*, 119–20; Klein, "Sündenverständnis und theologia crucis bei Paulus," in *Theologia Crucis-Signum Crucis*, 260–76.

144. Sanders, *Paul and Palestinian Judaism*, 442–47.

145. Dunn, *Romans 1–8*, 153–55; Dunn, *Theology of Paul the Apostle*, 354–66; Dunn, "New Perspective," 23–28.

146. Westerholm, *Perspectives Old and New on Paul*, 313–14. For other reasons for

own works, and Rom 4:4 refers to "one who works."[147] The desire or attempt to keep the law is not condemned by Paul. Rather, Paul criticized Jews for not keeping the law and even encouraged the desire to keep the law by saying that the doers of the law will be justified (Rom 2:13). Paul does not deal with Jewish nationalism by the words "works of the law" in Rom 3:20 as already mentioned. Thus James Dunn's sociological understanding of Paul's reason for rejecting "works of the law" is not persuasive. Sanders' "solution to plight" reasoning cannot be supported by the text. The thrust of Paul's argument in Rom 1:18—3:20 is that all human beings are under the wrath and judgment of God—"plight"—by their idolatry and disobedience of God's will, which is revealed to them by the natural law and the Mosaic law. The "solution" to this human "plight" is presented by Paul from Rom 3:21 on.[148] Furthermore, Sanders' "solution to plight" concept is not logically attractive. If the law is perfect to make people righteous before God as Sanders argues, logically there is no reason for the righteousness of God to be manifested "apart from the law" (Rom 3:21).

Still the most persuasive explanation why "works of the law" cannot save is the traditional one, which is expressed nicely by Seifrid: "The 'works of the law' are inadequate to save, because no-one fulfils all the demands of the law."[149] Human inability to keep the law perfectly has lain behind Paul's argument about human sinfulness and not being justified before God.[150] Since people cannot keep the law completely, their mouths are closed and all of them are held guilty before God (Rom 3:19). Due to the human inability to obey the law in every detail, the function of the law is not to save but to give knowledge of sin (Rom 3:20b).[151] Through the law people recognize what commands in the law were not kept and come to confess their being sinners who "fall short of the glory of God" (Rom 3:23). Paul's catena in 3:10–18 reveals that all human beings, Jews and Greeks, are sinners by their

---

rejecting Gaston's view, see Schreiner, *Romans*, 170.

147. Westerholm, *Perspectives Old and New on Paul*, 313.

148. Thielman also argues that in Romans Paul presents his gospel with the plight-solution framework. See Thielman, *From Plight to Solution*, 87–116.

149. Seifrid, *Christ, Our Righteousness*, 102.

150. This view is supported by Schreiner. Schreiner, "Paul and Perfect Obedience to the Law," 263.

151. Jeffrey A. D. Weima nicely analyzes the function of the law in three categories: (1) a cognitive function [Rom 3:20; 7:7; Gal 3:19]; (2) a converting function [Rom 5:13; 4:15]; and (3) a causative function [Rom 7:5, 8–11; 5:20; 1 Cor 15:56]. Rom 3:20b represents a cognitive function of the law in regard to sin. As Weima contends, "the law reveals to humanity its true sinful condition," acting "as a spiritual mirror." Weima, "Function of the Law in Relation to Sin," 219–35, esp. 223–24.

violating the law, which speaks to them and provides "knowledge of sin" (Rom 3:9, 19, 20b).

In summary, who will not be justified by works of the law in Rom 3:20? Does Paul have only Jews in mind by "no flesh" and does he say that Jews will not be saved by their particular works of the law, which are done as boundary markers? Or otherwise, does he proclaim that all human beings, Jews and gentiles, will not be saved by works of the law? Although some scholars, especially the proponents of the New Perspective, believe that in Rom 3:20 Paul speaks about the Jews and their exclusive keeping of some specific commandments of the Mosaic law, Rom 3:20 denotes that Paul teaches all human beings' inability to be justified by keeping the law. Paul has placed both Jews and gentiles under the law in Rom 1:18—3:19 and has proven their being sinners. Now he concludes in Rom 3:20 that no one, Jew or gentile, can be justified by the works of the law, since no one can keep the law perfectly. Although Jews and gentiles have access to the law, neither of them can be saved ("justified") by the works of the law. They simply remain silenced by finding out their sinfulness according to the "knowledge of sin" coming from the law. Because of human inability to be justified by works of the law, Christ came to be our righteousness.

ROMANS 3:21–31: JUSTIFIED GENTILES BY FAITH IN CHRIST

Paul proclaimed in Rom 3:19–20 that gentiles as well as Jews cannot be justified by works of the law but are silent before God by recognizing their sinfulness in the light of the law. In Rom 3:21–26, Paul now proclaims how people can be justified.

Not by Works of the Law, but through Faith in Christ (Rom 3:21–22, 26)

Paul emphasizes in Rom 3:21 that the righteousness of God has been manifested *apart from the law* (χωρὶς νόμου). The expression "apart from the law" reminds us of the previous verse. Human beings cannot be justified by works of the law and the law provides only knowledge of sin (Rom 3:20). Such failure of the law as a means of justification, which is due to human inability to keep the law perfectly, requires another way of justification, which is "apart from the law."

This alternative way is not based on human works but on God's grace (Rom 3:24, 4:4); thus it is asserted that "the righteousness *of God* (δικαιοσύνη θεοῦ, Rom 3:21) has been manifested." The righteousness to save human beings from the wrath of God is not human beings' righteousness, since the righteousness to save cannot be found in human beings as Paul has already proclaimed in Rom 3:10, thinking probably of Ps 14:1, 3 (13:1, 3 LXX) and Eccl 7:20: "There is none righteous, not even one."[152]

A parallel expression can be found in Phil 3:9. Paul confesses there that his righteousness is not his own (μὴ ἔχων ἐμὴν δικαιοσύνην), which derives *from the law* (τὴν ἐκ νόμου), but the righteousness which comes *from God* (τὴν ἐκ θεοῦ δικαιοσύνην). As Phil 3:9 talks of the righteousness that comes not from the law, the righteousness Paul deals with in Rom 3:21 is also the righteousness that can be manifested apart from the law. As Phil 3:9 mentions not Paul's own righteousness coming from the law, but the righteousness from God, so Rom 3:21 states not the righteousness of human beings but the righteousness of God. Human beings' own righteousness is impossible because all, both Jews and gentiles, have sinned (Rom 3:23) under the power of sin (Rom 3:9).[153]

Romans 3:22 explains that God's righteousness is available through faith in Jesus Christ (διὰ πίστεως Ἰησοῦ Χριστοῦ)—rather than relying on works of the law—to all who believe (εἰς πάντας τοὺς πιστεύοντας)—rather than for all who work. God's righteousness is for *all* (πάντας) who *believe* in Christ.[154] The word πάντας means all human beings who believe, not just Jewish believers.[155] The righteousness of God is thus available to both Jewish and gentile believers. In this sense, Rom 3:22b contends that God is impartial. Romans 3:25 again presents "faith" as an instrument to be justified (διὰ [τῆς] πίστεως, "through faith"). Romans 3:26 asserts that God justifies the one who has faith in Jesus (τὸν ἐκ πίστεως Ἰησοῦ). Just as Paul explained *all human beings'* sinfulness and their inability to be saved by works of the law,

---

152. According to Seifrid, Paul in Rom 3:10 rephrases Ps 13:1 and 3 LXX, having Eccl 7:20 ("There is no righteous person on earth") in mind. Seifrid, "Romans," 616.

153. Being under sin (ὑφ' ἁμαρτίαν, Rom 3:9) implies being under the power of sin as well as doing sinful acts. Human beings' fundamental problem with sin is not only doing sinful acts against the law but being kept under the power of sin and being reigned by sin (Rom 5:21). By the Holy Spirit, human beings can be free from the power of sin and can obey God's commandments. For the issue of the power of sin and bondage to sin, see Schreiner, *Romans*, 164; Schreiner, *New Testament Theology*, 534–38.

154. The words "all who believe (πάντας τοὺς πιστεύοντας)" entail the question: believe whom/what? Paul seems to provide the object of the belief in his previous words πίστεως Ἰησοῦ Χριστοῦ. Thus "Jesus Christ" is used as the object of faith. Righteousness of God is for all who believe in Christ.

155. Fitzmyer, *Romans*, 346; Schreiner, *Romans*, 184.

so Paul now proclaims *all human beings'* possibility to be justified through faith in Jesus Christ.

Paul juxtaposes works of the law and faith in Christ "as mutually exclusive ways of seeking God's righteousness."[156] Paul describes universal condemnation and salvation in terms of the contrast between works of the law and faith in Christ. For Paul, "apart from the law, through faith in Christ" is a principle applicable to all human beings, since all people are under the law and suffer from the inability to keep the whole law and from being guilty. "Through faith in Christ" is good news to those who are under the law and fail to be justified by works of the law. And it is indeed good news to all human beings because all of them, Jews and gentiles, are sinners under the law and fall short of the glory of God (Rom 3:23).

God's Righteousness for Gentiles as Well as Jews

In Rom 3:21–26 Paul explains God's righteousness, which has been manifested apart from the law and witnessed by the Old Testament. One of the characteristics of Paul's statement in this part is that God takes the center stage. *God's* righteousness is mentioned four times in verses 21, 22, 25, and 26. People fall short of the glory *of God* (v. 23). People are justified by *God's* grace as a gift (v. 24). *God* set forth Christ as a ἱλαστήριον (v. 25).[157] Paul's focus is especially on God's righteousness, which remains intact in God's justifying the unrighteous and in his judging the world righteously as a righteous judge (cf. 3:5–6). God's righteousness manifested on the cross of Christ, thus, can be explained as saving and judging righteousness.[158] Whereas Rom 3:21–22 primarily reveals God's saving righteousness, Rom 3:25–26 largely reveals God's judging righteousness.[159]

God's saving righteousness is the forensic declaration in the divine court that those who believe are just despite their being sinners in terms of their works of the law. God's saving righteousness is historically based on Christ's death on a cross. Romans 3:24 witnesses that Jews and gentiles are justified "through the redemption [διὰ τῆς ἀπολυτρώσεως] which is in Christ Jesus." Redemption (ἀπολύτρωσις) implies paying a price or a ransom

156. Moo, "'Law', 'Works of the Law', and Legalism in Paul," 74.

157. Byrne correctly finds the initiative of God in setting forth Christ as a ἱλαστήριον. Byrne, *Romans*, 126.

158. For the meaning of God's righteousness, see Schreiner, *Romans*, 63–69. He contends that in Rom 3:21–26 "the righteousness of God involves both his saving and judging righteousness."

159. Schreiner, *Romans*, 68.

(λύτρον) to liberate slaves from bondage.[160] Carson, referring to Rom 3:9, points out that Paul has already said that "sin . . . has not only made all human beings judicially guilty before God, but it has enslaved them."[161] According to Carson, Christ's death is the price paid to emancipate human beings from the slavery of sin and to free them from "death that is nothing other than sin's penalty."[162]

Christ's death reflects God's judging righteousness. As Thielman correctly understands, God's "character as a righteous judge of the world" is preserved through the death of Christ on a cross.[163] All human beings are under the wrath and judgment of God because of their failure to keep the law of God (Rom 1:18, 2:5, 3:5). Christ died for gentiles as well as Jews to save them from the wrath and punishment of God by his atoning sacrifice. In this regard, Paul identifies Christ as a ἱλαστήριον in Rom 3:25. Scholars have debated regarding the meaning of ἱλαστήριον. Many scholars reject finding the concept of propitiation from this word by defending the concept of expiation. However, both concepts do not necessarily exclude each other. Christ is the ultimate mercy seat where sins are expiated and the wrath of God is propitiated.

Romans 3:25 makes it clear that the blood poured for expiation and propitiation is the blood of Christ (ἐν τῷ αὐτοῦ αἵματι, "in his blood"). The sacrificial system in the old covenant is a shadow of Christ's sacrificial death on a cross. By looking forward to Christ's blood, the Old Testament's sacrificial system atoned for people's sin. Moo explains this as follows:

> By referring to Christ as this "mercy seat," then, Paul would be inviting us to view Christ as the New Covenant equivalent, or antitype, to this Old Covenant "place of atonement," and, derivatively, to the ritual of atonement itself. What in the OT was hidden from public view behind the veil has now been "publicly displayed" as the OT ritual is fulfilled and brought to an end in Christ's "once-for-all" sacrifice.

God passed over (πάρεσις) former sins in his forbearance because he anticipated Christ's atoning death. If Christ had not been set forth as a ἱλαστήριον, God would have been found as an unrighteous judge in his passing over sins. But Paul contends in Rom 3:26 that God's righteousness has been proved (ἔνδειξις) by Christ's death. Because of Christ's atoning death for sinners, God justifies by grace all Jews and gentiles who have faith

---

160. Schreiner, *Romans*, 189–90; Carson, "Why Trust a Cross?" 353.

161. Carson, "Why Trust a Cross?," 353.

162. Carson, "Why Trust a Cross?," 353.

163. Thielman, *Theology of the New Testament*, 353.

in Jesus (saving righteousness), and preserves his righteousness as the righteous judge who punishes sinners (judging righteousness).

In Rom 3:21–26, Paul's focus is on how people who cannot be justified by works of the law can be justified. All who believe can be justified according to Paul. Paul's argument about human beings' justification has been made by the contrast between works of the law and faith in Christ. No flesh can be justified by works of the law since no one can keep the law perfectly. Paul's assertion that no flesh can be justified by works of the law in Rom 3:20 is rephrased by Paul as that all have sinned and fall short of the glory of God in Rom 3:23. Both "no flesh" and "all" mean Jews and gentiles. Paul first proves *by the law* that all human beings, gentiles as well as Jews, are sinners and cannot escape from the wrath and righteous judgment of God. To explain the gospel, in which the righteousness of God is revealed (Rom 1:17) to gentile believers in Rome, Paul places gentiles along with Jews under the law and shows their need of God's righteousness, which is available through faith in Christ, not by works of the law, for all who believe (Rom 3:22).

ROMANS 6:14–15

Paul states in Rom 6:14a that "sin shall not be master over you." The reason for this statement is explained in 6:14b as γάρ indicates: "because (γάρ) you are not under law, but under grace."[164] In 6:15, Paul questions whether being not under law but under grace can be a pretense for sinning: "Shall we sin because we are not under law but under grace?" Paul's answer is "may it never be (μὴ γένοιτο)!"

In this passage, human beings' new life in Christ is explained by Paul in terms of their new status, that is, not being under law but being under grace. Freedom from the mastering power of sin is due to Christians' liberation from being under law. As Moo rightly observes, Paul employs in Rom 6:17–23 "his customary 'once . . . but now' device to contrast his readers' pre-Christian existence with their Christian experience."[165] Moo explains Paul's contrast regarding "once . . . but now" noted in verses 17–23, saying "'once' they (Roman Christians) were slaves of sin, doing shameful things that led to death; 'now' they are slaves of God and of righteousness, and do things that lead to holiness and life."[166]

---

164. Schreiner also understands v. 14b "gives a reason why (γάρ) sin shall not exercise its tyranny over us." Schreiner, *Romans*, 325.

165. Moo, *Epistle to the Romans*, 397.

166. Moo, *Epistle to the Romans*, 397.

This "once . . . but now" contrast shows that in Paul's mind Roman Christians (predominantly gentiles) were previously *under law* and were mastered by sin. Now they are no longer under law; therefore, they are free from sin's tyranny. Paul's explanation of gentile Christians' new life is based on his understanding that gentiles were previously under law despite their being without the Mosaic law, which was bestowed to the Jews on Mount Sinai. Martin also supports this interpretation by saying, "At Rom 6:14 the reason sin will not now act as Lord over the Roman Christians is that they are not *hypo nomon* but *hypo charin*. The implication is that previously they were not *hypo charin* but *hypo nomon* and *hyph' hamartian* (cf Rom 3:9; and Rom 6)."[167]

In Rom 6:14–15, then what law does Paul have in mind? It is hard to determine whether Paul refers to the Mosaic law or law in general. While Hodge and Murray understand the law to be law in general,[168] Fitzmyer, Moo, and Schreiner think it to be the Mosaic law.[169] Hodge contends:

> By *law* here, is not to be understood the Mosaic law. The sense is not, 'Sin shall not have dominion over you, because the Mosaic law is abrogated.' The word is to be taken in its widest sense. It is the rule of duty, that which binds the conscience as an expression of the will of God.[170]

He further provides four reasons for seeing the law in Rom 6:14 as law in general rather than the Mosaic law:

> 1. From the use of the word through this epistle and other parts of the New Testament. 2. From the whole doctrine of redemption, which teaches that the law from which we are delivered by the death of Christ, is not simply the Mosaic law; we are not merely delivered from Judaism, but from the obligation of fulfilling the law of God as the condition of salvation. 3. Deliverance from the Mosaic law does not secure holiness. A man may cease to be a Jew, and yet not be a new creature in Christ Jesus. 4. The antithesis between law and grace shows that more than the law of Moses is here intended. If free from the Mosaic law, they may still be under some other law, and as little under grace as the Pharisees.

167. Martin, *Christ and the Law in Paul*, 101.

168. Hodge, *Commentary on Romans*, 205–206; Murray, *Epistle to the Romans*, 1:228–29.

169. Fitzmyer, *Romans*, 447; Moo, *Epistle to the Romans*, 387–89; Schreiner, *Romans*, 325.

170. Hodge, *Commentary on Romans*, 205. Italics original.

Hodge's conclusion is that "to be under the law is to be under the obligation to fulfill the law of God as a rule of duty, as the condition of salvation."

Regarding the law in Rom 6:14, Murray contends that it "must be understood in the general sense of law as law."[171] His rationale for this position is described as follows:

> That it [law] is not to be understood in the sense of the Mosaic law as an economy appears plainly from the fact that many who were under the Mosaic economy were the recipients of grace and in that regard were under the grace, and also from the fact that relief from the Mosaic law as an economy does not of itself place persons in the category of being under grace.[172]

For Murray, law is therefore understood "in much more general terms of law as commandment."[173] If Hodge and Murray are correct, when Paul places pre-Christian gentiles under law in Rom 6:14–15, he means that he has in mind more general law rather than the Mosaic law.

On the other hand, Moo understands the law to be the Mosaic law. He believes that Paul presents his gospel from the perspective of Old Covenant and New. Paul, according to Moo, describes here the Mosaic law in terms of its condemning effect in the Old Covenant.[174] For Moo, "to be 'under the law' means to be subject to the curse of the law that comes because of the inevitable failure to accomplish the law (cf. 3:19–20; Gal. 3:10–14)."[175] In addition, Moo understands Paul to be contrasting "law" and "grace" in terms of salvation-historical "powers" and "realms."[176] To be "under law" is to be subject to the old age when the Mosaic law rules, whereas "to be 'under grace' is to be subject to the new age in which freedom from the power of sin is available."[177]

Schreiner regards the word νόμος as the Mosaic law as well.[178] His interpretation of Rom 6:14 is as follows:

> The phrases ὑπὸ νόμον and ὑπὸ χάριν . . . are best understood in a salvation-historical sense . . . . They refer to different eras in God's redemptive historical plan. The term ὑπὸ νόμον designates

---

171. Murray, *Epistle to the Romans*, 1:228.

172. Murray, *Epistle to the Romans*, 1:228–29.

173. Murray, *Epistle to the Romans*, 1:229.

174. Moo, *Epistle to the Romans*, 387–89.

175. Moo, *Epistle to the Romans*, 388.

176. Moo, *Epistle to the Romans*, 389.

177. Moo, *Epistle to the Romans*, 389.

178. Schreiner, *Romans*, 325.

the Mosaic era as a whole, while ὑπὸ χάριν describes the new age inaugurated through the death and resurrection of Jesus Christ. The logic of verse 14 is as follows: If you were still under the era of law, then sin would rule over you; since you are under the age of grace, sin cannot have dominion over you. I conclude from this that Paul is saying that to live under the Mosaic covenant was to live under the power of sin.[179]

Although there are different voices among scholars regarding the meaning of the word νόμος, it is apparent that Paul places pre-Christian gentiles under *law*. They are enslaved to sin under law (Rom 6:6). Paul places all human beings either under grace or under law, although gentiles did not receive the Mosaic law. Calvin clearly understands that in Paul's mind all people, Jews and gentiles, are under law and its condemnation, as his comment on Rom 6:14 shows:

> We are to understand here, moreover, that the apostle takes it for granted that all those who are without the grace of God are bound by the yoke of the law, and held under its condemnation.[180]

ROMANS 7:4–6

In Rom 7:1–3, Paul speaks about the freedom of a married woman from her husband in his death. A married woman can marry another man without being accused of adultery when her husband dies because "she is released from the law concerning the husband" (κατήργηται ἀπὸ τοῦ νόμου, Rom 7:2). Following this illustration, Paul states that Roman Christians "have been released from the law" (κατηργήθημεν ἀπὸ τοῦ νόμου, Rom 7:6) by being "put to death to the law through the body of Christ" (Rom 7:4). Now they can bear fruit not for death but for God (Rom 7:4, 5) and "serve in newness of Spirit and not oldness of letter" (Rom 7:6).

Paul's notion that gentiles are under the law can be found here in Rom 7:4–6. In Paul's mind, pre-Christian Roman gentiles must have been bound under the law and needed to be released from it in order to serve in the new life of the Spirit. Had they not been bound, they would never have been released. This interpretation can be supported by the marriage illustration that Paul used. The woman who can be released from the law regarding her husband needs to be formerly bound to the law by living with her husband when he was alive. Pre-Christian Roman gentiles were

179. Schreiner, *Romans*, 326.

180. Calvin, *Epistle of Paul the Apostle to the Romans and to the Thessalonians*, 131.

under the law when they were living in the flesh (ἐν τῇ σαρκι, v. 5). Their sinful passions were aroused by *the law* and resulted in bearing fruit for death (Rom 7:5). Martin also supports the view that Paul places gentiles under law in Rom 7:4–6 by saying:

> At Rom 7:4–6 before the Roman Christians could belong to Christ, bear fruit for God, or serve in the new life of the Spirit, they first had to be set free from the law and die to the law. Previously they were in the flesh and their sinful passions were aroused by the law and bore fruit for death (7:5).[181]

ROMANS 8:3–4

Νόμος in Rom 8:3–4 is the Mosaic law.[182] In verse 3, Paul states the inability of the law to make people stand righteous before God and break sin's tyranny.[183] The reason is that the law is weak through the flesh. Paul does not say that the law has a problem in itself. For Paul, the law is holy, just, and good (Rom 7:12). The problem is with human beings who cannot keep the law perfectly. The law cannot be obeyed completely because of human beings' corrupted nature inherited from Adam.[184] All human beings are under the condemnation of the law and fall short of the glory of God (cf. Rom 8:1; 3:23).

God has done what the law could not do. He sent his own son and made him an offering for sin (περὶ ἁμαρτίας).[185] Christ's sacrificial death for sin sets those who are in Christ Jesus free from the condemnation of the law and provides righteousness (Rom 8:1). In verse 4 the purpose of God's sending his son is formulated in this phrase, "that the requirement of *the law* might be fulfilled in *us*" (ἵνα τὸ δικαίωμα τοῦ νόμου πληρωθῇ ἐν ἡμῖν).

Romans 8:3–4 proves that Paul places gentiles under the law. Christ was condemned as a substitute for Roman Christians who were under the requirement of the Law, but unable to fulfill it perfectly. Christ fulfilled what

181. Martin, *Christ and the Law in Paul*, 101.

182. Moo, *Epistle to the Romans*, 478.

183. Moo understands "what the law could not do" negatively as "to break sin's power" and positively as "to secure eschatological life." Moo, *Epistle to the Romans*, 478.

184. Schreiner correctly mentions that "the weakness of the law is located in flesh, the unregenerate nature of human beings." Schreiner, *Romans*, 401.

185. The words περὶ ἁμαρτίας in Rom 8:3 are understood as "an offering for sin" by Calvin. So also by many significant scholars. See Calvin, *Epistle of Paul the Apostle to the Romans and to the Thessalonians*, 159–60; Wilckens, *Der Brief an die Römer*, 2:127; Dunn, *Romans 1–8*, 422; Schreiner, *Romans*, 403; Wright, *Letter to the Romans*, 579.

the law required and set gentile Christians free from the law of sin and death (Rom 8:2). The law no longer lays claim to the condemnation of gentile Christians because the condemnation has already been taken in the flesh of Christ (ἐν τῇ σαρκί, Rom 8:3). Paul places lawless gentiles under the law and explains his gospel accordingly.

CONCLUSION

In this chapter, we have seen from Romans that Paul places lawless gentiles under the law. In Rom 1:18–32, in which Paul claims gentiles' sinfulness, Paul argues that gentiles know God and his will from his creation. Gentiles hear the Mosaic law's moral norms through the natural law. Therefore, they are under the wrath of God without excuse for their idolatry and other sins originating from it. They are even aware of the death penalty which the law prescribes on sinners (Rom 1:32).

Although gentiles do not have the law, Paul places them under the law since they are the law to themselves (Rom 2:14). Paul employs the natural-law concept to explain why they are the law to themselves (Rom 2:15): Lawless gentiles "do by nature the things of the law"; the work of the law is written in the hearts of gentiles; and their conscience witnesses and thoughts accuse or excuse. By placing gentiles under the law, Paul proves that Jews do not find the favor of God simply because of their having the written law of God. According to Paul, gentiles also have the law despite their lack of the written law of Moses. Thus, Paul claims that not hearers but doers of the law will be justified before God.

Romans 3:19 indicates that Paul includes gentiles within the category of "those who are in the law," to whom the law speaks. Paul places gentiles along with Jews in the sphere of the law, which refers to the Old Testament in the case of Rom 3:19. This explains why Paul uses the Jewish Scriptures authoritatively with gentiles in Romans and in his other letters. Because the law speaks to Gentiles as well as to Jews, every mouth is stopped and all the world is held guilty before God.

Paul's declaration that no flesh will be justified before God by works of the law (Rom 3:20) should not be understood as Paul's address exclusively to the Jews in terms of their circumcision and keeping Sabbath and purity laws. The message of Rom 3:19 and the words διότι and πᾶσα σάρξ in 3:20 indicate that Paul relates "works of the law" to all humans beings, not just to Jews. Some scholars try to limit Paul's address in Rom 3:20 to the Jewish people on the grounds that the law in this verse means the Jewish law. However, they fail to understand that Paul places gentiles under the Mosaic law to prove gentiles' sinfulness and their hopelessness in being saved by works of the law.

Romans 3:21–31 is God's solution to human beings' inability to be justified by works of the law. People can be justified before God only through faith in Christ. The righteousness of God is available to all who believe in Christ, because Christ died on the cross as a ἱλαστήριον. "Through faith in Christ" is good news to all human beings, Jews and gentiles, who could not be justified by works under the law.

Romans 6:14–15, 7:4–6, and 8:3–4 additionally indicate that Paul places gentiles under the law. Gentile Christians in Rome were previously under law, but they are now under grace. They were bound under the law but are now released from it. Sin no longer controls Roman Christian who died to the law in Christ. Gentiles as well as Jews were under the requirement of the law and were unable to fulfill it perfectly. God sent his own Son in order that the requirement of the law might be fulfilled in gentiles as well as in Jews.

Although Paul acknowledges that the Mosaic law is an ethnic privilege originally given to the Jews on Mount Sinai, he places gentiles along with Jews under the law in Romans. The Mosaic law is an instrument Paul employs to explain his gospel to gentiles.

CHAPTER 4

Gentiles under the Curse of
the Law in Galatians

INTRODUCTION

How does Paul understand the relationship between the law and gentiles? Do gentiles have nothing to do with the law because the law was given to Jews on Mount Sinai? In this chapter we will investigate Galatians to see that Paul places gentiles under the law. In Galatians, Paul explains his gospel by placing lawless gentiles (cf. Rom 2:12, 9:4) under the law and, especially, under its curse. The purpose of Christ's incarnation and death on the cross is to redeem those who are under the law from the curse of the law (Gal 3:13, 4:4–5). Although the Mosaic law was given to Israel as their ethnic privilege on Mount Sinai at a certain time in salvation history (cf. Gal 3:17, "which came four hundred and thirty years later"), for Paul no one is free from the curse of the law. All human beings, Jews or gentiles, are under the law and its curse. Therefore, all human beings need Christ who redeems them from the curse. In this chapter, we will observe how Paul explains his gospel to gentiles by placing them under the law and its curse and how Paul interprets Christ's death on the cross for gentiles' salvation. If one misses the point that Paul places gentiles under the law and its curse, consequently, the meaning of Christ's death can be misunderstood. Paul's soteriology for gentiles can be properly understood when one understands Paul placing gentiles under the law and its curse.

ALL HUMAN BEINGS ARE UNDER THE CURSE OF THE LAW (GAL 3:10–12)

In Gal 3:10, Paul states that "as many as are of the works of the Law are under a curse (Ὅσοι ἐξ ἔργων νόμου εἰσίν, ὑπὸ κατάραν εἰσίν), for it is written, 'Cursed is everyone who does not abide by all things written in the book of the law, to do them.'" In this verse, Paul puts all human beings, whether Jews or gentiles, under the curse of the law by the words "as many as" (ὅσοι). The reason why all human beings are inevitably under the curse of the law can be found in their inability to obey the whole law perfectly.[1] Thomas Schreiner explains human inability as the reason for the curse by detecting an implicit premise in Gal 3:10 as follows:

> Those who do not keep everything written in the law are cursed (3:10b).
> No one keeps everything written in the law (implicit premise).
> Therefore, those who rely on the works of the law for salvation are cursed (3:10a).[2]

Human beings fail to achieve perfect obedience because they are unable to keep the law perfectly both in the quantitative and qualitative aspects.[3]

From the fact that no one can keep the law in its entirety, Paul moves to a logical conclusion that "no one is justified before God *by the law*" (Gal 3:11). "No one" (οὐδείς) signifies that all human beings, both Jews and gentiles, cannot be justified by the law, because of their common inability to keep the law perfectly. The citation of Hab 2:4 evidences that works of the law cannot be used for the justification of human beings, because "the righteous man shall live *by faith*" rather than *the law*.

For Paul, righteousness by works of the law is unattainable not because the law itself has any defect, nor because the desire to obey the law is sinful, as Rudolf Bultmann posits.[4] The law is holy, righteous, and good (Rom 7:12). The doers of the law will be justified (Rom 2:13). Then, the problem is not the law but the people who are supposed to obey the law.[5] Due to the

---

1. A similar notion that one needs to keep all things written in the book of the law in order not to be a transgressor of the law is found in Jas 2:11: "For He who said, 'Do not commit adultery,' also said, 'Do not commit murder.' Now if you do not commit adultery, but do commit murder, you have become a transgressor of the law."

2. Schreiner, *Law and Its Fulfillment*, 44.

3. Regarding the qualitative aspect of Gal 3:10, see Laato, "Paul's Anthropological Considerations," 357–59.

4. Bultmann, *Theology of the New Testament*, 1:264.

5. Laato correctly points out that "in accordance with Deuteronomy 27:26, Paul maintains elsewhere that the curse is not related to the Torah in and of itself, but to

lack of human beings' power to keep the law (Gal 3:10, cf. Rom 8:3), the law given to human beings cannot be considered as a life-giving law (Gal 3:21). Otherwise, as Paul states in Gal 3:21, righteousness would have been by the law and, as Paul states in Gal 2:21, Christ can be considered as having died in vain.[6] The law cannot function as a way of justification for human beings. That is why Christ died on the cross. For Paul, to insist upon the possibility of justification through the law is to nullify the grace of God (ἀθετῶ τὴν χάριν τοῦ θεοῦ, Gal 2:21). The grace of God in sending Christ for sinners was necessary only because there was no other way to save sinners. The grace of God can be rightly appreciated only when one understands his or her hopelessness in being justified by the law. The law condemns and keeps people under the curse of the law as long as they fail to obey the law in its totality. Since they cannot keep the law perfectly, human beings cannot be liberated from the curse of the law.

ONLY JEWS ARE UNDER THE CURSE OF THE LAW?

Contrary to this book's interpretation on Gal 3:10 that Paul denotes that all human beings including gentiles are under the curse of the law because of their falling short of complete obedience to the law, some scholars try to put only Jews under the curse of the law by interpreting the phrase "works of the law" as Jewish identity markers such as circumcision, food laws, and the Sabbath. James Dunn claims "works of the law" to be Jewish practice of the law to maintain covenant righteousness.[7] In other words, "works of the law" represents a Jewish lifestyle separating Jews from gentiles.[8] Thus, according to Dunn, "ὅσοι ἐξ ἔργων νόμου are Jews as a whole, precisely insofar as they understand themselves in terms of the law."[9] Jews are under the curse because they misunderstand God's plan to include gentiles as sharers of Abraham's blessing and continue to insist on Israel's privilege, "shutting out" gentiles.[10]

(evil!) works (cf. Rom 2:12; 4:15; 7:10–11; 1 Cor 15:56)." Laato, "Paul's Anthropological Considerations," 355.

6. Gal 3:21 clearly opposes Sanders' view that Paul did not see any problem with the law. According to Sanders, the law was perfect to save but Paul rejected it because he found Christ to be the solution. Galatians 3:21, however, states that "if a law had been given which was able to impart life, then righteousness would indeed have been based on law." Sanders, *Paul and Palestinian Judaism*, 442–47.

7. Dunn, *Theology of Paul the Apostle*, 359–66.

8. Dunn, *Romans 1–8*, 154–55; Dunn, *Epistle to the Galatians*, 172.

9. Dunn, "Works of the Law and the Curse of the Law," 533–34.

10. Dunn, *Theology of Paul the Apostle*, 361–62; Dunn, *Epistle to the Galatians*,

Dunn's interpretation, however, cannot be sustained in the light of Gal 3:13. If Dunn's case is correct, Gal 3:13 has to mean that the curse from which Christ redeemed "us" by his death on the cross is simply Jewish misunderstanding of the law and the Jews' wrong attitude, which excludes gentiles from the covenant promise. Actually, Dunn explains Gal 3:13 in that way:

> The curse of the law here has to do primarily with the attitude which confines the covenant promise to Jews as Jews: it falls on those who live within the law in such a way as to exclude the Gentiles as Gentiles from the promise. . . . The curse which was removed therefore by Christ's death was the curse which had previously prevented that blessing from reaching the Gentiles, the curse of a wrong understanding of the law. It was a curse which fell primarily on the Jew (3.10; 4.5), but Gentiles were affected by it so long as that misunderstanding of the covenant and the law remained dominant. It was that curse which Jesus had brought deliverance from by his death.[11]

As Dunn himself acknowledges, this is "a surprisingly narrow understanding of the redemptive effect of Christ's death."[12] Did Christ die indeed to correct Jews' wrong attitude toward gentiles and their misunderstanding of the law? Furthermore, if only Jews are ὅσοι ἐξ ἔργων νόμου and are under the curse of the law in Gal 3:10 due to their exclusivism, those who are redeemed from the curse (i.e., "us") in Gal 3:13 should be Jews. Strangely, however, Dunn interprets "us" in Gal 3:13 to be Jews and gentiles.[13] If Gal 3:13 denotes that Christ redeemed Jews and gentiles from the curse of the law, ὅσοι ἐξ ἔργων νόμου and those who are under the curse of the law in Gal 3:10 should be Jews and gentiles as well. Regarding this problem with Dunn's interpretation, Seyoon Kim legitimately questions:

> The Jews are then liberated from the curse they received from the law for their nationalism. But then how are the gentiles liberated from the curse? Did they have any "curse of the law" in the sense of Dunn's interpretation, in the first place? Or did they also have the Jewish nationalism so as to incur "the curse of the law" in the sense of verse 10 as interpreted by Dunn?[14]

170–74.

11. Dunn, "Works of the Law and the Curse of the Law," 536.

12. Dunn, "Works of the Law and the Curse of the Law," 536.

13. Dunn, *Epistle to the Galatians*, 176–77.

14. Seyoon Kim, *Paul and the New Perspective*, 132.

Paul seems not to use "works of the law" in Gal 3:10 as a symbol of Jewish efforts to exclude gentiles, but to use them as human beings' efforts in general to obtain justification. Of course, Jews are included in ὅσοι ἐξ ἔργων νόμου since their keeping the Mosaic law can be "works" as well. Nevertheless, the idea that only Jews are ὅσοι ἐξ ἔργων νόμου and are under the curse of the law cannot be maintained. All human beings, including gentiles, are under the law and its curse. Jews and gentiles, as Dunn rightly observes, are redeemed from the curse of the law (Gal 3:13). The reason for their being under the curse of the law is their not keeping the law perfectly.

Richard B. Hays, who considers "ἡμᾶς" in Gal 3:13 to be referring to Jews, renders "those who are of the works of the law" (v. 10) as "those whose identity is derived from works of Law."[15] Since it is Jews who identify themselves by works of the law and who are under the curse of the law in Gal 3:10, for Hays gentiles cannot be under the curse of the law in Gal 3:13. In Gal 3:10–12, however, Paul does not use "works of the law" to refer to only Jewish identity markers, nor does Paul say that Jews who exclude gentiles from God's people by emphasizing their ethnic privileges will be under a curse. The reason for the curse presented in Gal 3:10 is failing to keep "all things (πᾶσιν)" written in the book of the law. If Paul connects "works" to "all things written," the "works of the law" cannot be restricted to the boundary makers. In this regard, A. Andrew Das's comment is insightful:

> Paul's citation in Gal 3:10 shows that he has in mind by the phrase "works of the law" more than just the ethnic aspects of the law. Deuteronomy 27–30 is full of curses against all sorts of legal violations: illicit sexual relations, misleading the blind, changing borders, following other gods, even withholding justice from widows and orphans.[16]

James M. Scott also points out that Dunn's "interpretation of 'works of the law' ignores the fact that Deut. 27.26 refers to 'all' the commandments of the law, not just to certain 'badges' of Jewish nationalism."[17] "Works of the law" refers to doing all things the law prescribes.

Paul's argument is not about the issue of gentiles' inclusion or exclusion in Judaism. The subject of his argument is rather about justification by faith. In other words, he talks about "works of the law" and "faith in Christ" as two competitive ways for justification. For Paul, even Jews are not insiders if they are not justified by faith in Christ despite their works of the law (Gal 2:16) including circumcision and keeping food laws. All human

15. Hays, *Letter to the Galatians*, 257.

16. Das, *Paul, the Law, and the Covenant*, 157.

17. Scott, "'For as Many as Are of Works of the Law Are under a Curse,'" 192.

beings, Jews or gentiles, are equal in terms of their becoming people of God in the new era dawned by Christ. Jews are not the default people of God. According to Paul, "neither is circumcision anything, nor uncircumcision, but a new creation" (Gal 6:12). The "Israel of God" is redefined by Paul as those who are a new creation in Christ (Gal 6:15–16, cf. 2 Cor 5:17).

Paul rejects "works of the law" but not because it separated gentiles from Jews. The gentiles' separation from Jews is not Paul's concern since "Israel of God" refers to neither Jews nor gentiles but those who are in Christ. The reason for Paul's rejection of human works of the law is that works of the law cannot make Jews and gentiles stand righteous before God, because their works of the law cannot be perfect.

The body hanged on a tree is said to be accursed of God in Deut 21:23. However, the text never implies that his being cursed has something to do with preventing gentiles from being accepted into the covenant people. His being cursed is related to "a sin worthy of death" (Deut 21:22). Paul's citation of Deut 27:26 asserts, "Cursed is everyone who does not abide by all things written in the book of the law, to perform them" (Gal 3:10). The curse depends on one's not keeping all things written in the book of the law rather than not keeping some regulations which prevent gentiles from being included in the Jewish community. In other words, curse is related to sin (Deut 21:22), which is interpreted as not keeping all things written in the book of the law (Gal: 3:10).

N. T. Wright provides an influential argument that only Jews are under the curse of the law in Gal 3:10. According to Wright, the curse of the law in Gal 3:10 is the exile of Israel and "the death of Jesus, precisely on a Roman cross which symbolized so clearly the continuing subjugation of the people of God, brought the exile to a climax."[18] Christ's redemptive death on the cross restores Israel from the exile and renews her covenantal relationship with God. Wright's ingenious exposition of Gal 3:10 and 13 based on Israel's exile-restoration scheme is well summarized in his following statement:

> Because the Messiah represents Israel, he is able to take on himself Israel's curse and exhaust it. Jesus dies as the King of the Jews, at the hands of the Romans whose oppression of Israel is the present, and climactic, form of the curse of exile itself. The crucifixion of the Messiah is, one might say, the *quintessence of* the curse of exile, and its climactic act. The context thus demands the first person plural for which Paul has been criticized by some and misunderstood by others: he is not here producing a general statement of atonement theology applicable equally, and in the

18. Wright, *Climax of the Covenant*, 146.

same way, to Jew and Gentile alike. Christ, as the representative Messiah, has achieved a specific task, that of taking on himself the curse which hung over Israel and which on the one hand prevented her from enjoying full membership in Abraham's family and thereby on the other hand prevented the blessing of Abraham from flowing out to Gentiles. The Messiah has come where Israel is, under the Torah's curse (see 4.4), in order to be not only Israel's representative but Israel's redeeming representative.[19]

Wright argues that Gal 3:10–14 should be interpreted as referring to Israel's exile and restoration since Paul uses covenantal themes and covenantal words, such as "blessing" and "curse" in Gal 3:10–14 and Paul's citations are from the covenantal context of Gen 15 and Deut 27–30.[20] Thus, for Wright, Deut 27–30 is the basic context in which Gal 3:10–14 should be understood. Wright argues:

> In other words, Deuteronomy 27–30 is all about exile and restoration, *understood* as covenant judgment and covenant renewal. This, I suggest, is the basic context in which we can understand Galatians 3.10–14 in itself and in its relation to the rest of the chapter. In particular, 3.13 is not an isolated explanation of the cross, or a prooftext for justification by faith, or anything so atomistic. It is the sharp expression of a theme which occupies Paul throughout the chapter: the fact that in the cross of Jesus, the Messiah, the curse of exile itself reached its height, and was dealt with once for all, so that the blessing of covenant renewal might flow out the other side, as God always intended.[21]

However, whether the context of Deut 27–30 as Wright interprets, even if it is true, can be imposed on Gal 3:10–14 is questionable. Paul's citations of Deut 27:26 in Gal 3:10 and of Deut 21:23 in Gal 3:13 function to support Paul's argument in Galatians. In Gal 3:10–14, Paul is neither concerned about Israel's covenantal relationship with God nor her exile. He is simply interested in "what is written" as his connecting words γέγραπται in verse 10 (γέγραπται γὰρ ὅτι) and 13 (ὅτι γέγραπται) indicate. He proves his argument by citing the Old Testament scriptures. It is obvious that Paul does not mention Israel or anything implying Israel regarding his citations in Gal 3:10–14.[22] Although scholars' efforts to understand Paul's citation of

---

19. Wright, *Climax of the Covenant,* 151. Italics original.

20. Wright, *Climax of the Covenant,* 140–41.

21. Wright, *Climax of the Covenant,* 140–41. Italics original.

22. Some may argue that "works of the law" refer to Israel's religious life. However, it is not convincing.

Deut 27:26 in the context of the Old Testament and of Jewish traditions are basically meaningful, Paul is not likely to expect Galatian readers to probe into the original context of Paul's citation as modern scholars do to understand Paul to be referring to Israel's exile in Gal 3:10–14. The Galatian gentiles might have heard Paul's citation as it is and applied it to them. They might have considered the curse and redemption in Gal 3:10–14 as their curse and redemption rather than Israel's exile and restoration.

Paul's argument, thus, need not be distorted by pressing the context of the Old Testament too hard into a new context in which Paul cites the Old Testament. When we examine the function of Paul's citations in his argument in Gal 3:10–14, it is evident that Wright's speculation about Israel's exile is an unnecessary addition. Although the curse mentioned in Deut 27:26 is the covenantal curse applicable to Israel in their disobedience to the law, Paul's use of Deut 27:26 needs to be understood in the context of Gal 3:10 rather than that of Deut 27:26. The intention of Paul's citation of Deut 27:26 has been misunderstood by many scholars due to their excessive imposing of the context of Deuteronomy into Galatians.

Paul's intention to cite Deut 27:26 is to buttress his argument that all who are of the works of the law are under a curse. Paul does not explain Israel's curse or exile in Gal 3:10, nor does the context of Galatians 3:10–13 denote that Paul is discussing Israel's curse of exile and Christ's death for the restoration of Israel.

GENTILES UNDER THE LAW AND ITS CURSE IN GAL 3:10–12

On the other hand, there are some indications that Paul's statements in 3:10–12 are open to Jews and gentiles. The word ὅσοι in 3:10a ("as many as [ὅσοι] are of the works of the Law are under a curse") does not mean Jews exclusively. Seyoon Kim rightly argues:

> But then why did he [Paul] not write, "*Israel* [or *the Jews*] is under a curse," but instead, "*All those who* [ὅσοι] are of works of the law are under a curse"? In writing thus, he clearly sought to state something else than what his opponents and readers might have taken for granted. He wrote ὅσοι ἐξ ἔργων νόμου here rather than simply "the Jews" because he wanted to draw a generalized conclusion from the proof-text of Deuteronomy and apply it to others as well as the Jews.[23]

23. Kim, *Paul and the New Perspective*, 139. Italics original.

In addition, N. H. Young states that "Paul's use of ὅσοι elsewhere appears to be generally open in its term of reference," referring to Rom 6:3, 8:14, Gal 3:27, 6:12, 16; Phil 3:15 and Col 2:1.[24] The word πᾶς in 3:10b ("Cursed is everyone [πᾶς] who does not abide by all things written in the book of the law") does not mean Jews exclusively either.[25] Further, in Gal 3:11 Paul uses οὐδεὶς rather than "Jews": "Now that no one (οὐδεὶς) is justified by the Law before God is evident." "No one" here does not mean "no Jew." In Gal 3:12, Paul states, citing Lev 18:5, that "he who does them (ὁ ποιήσας αὐτα) will live." Bruce notes that the readers of this letter might have recalled τοῦ ποιῆσαι αὐτα ("to do them") in Gal 3:10 by αὐτα in 3:12 (ὁ ποιήσας αὐτα).[26] In 3:10, αὐτα, in τοῦ ποιῆσαι αὐτα ("to do them"), refers to "all things written in the book of the law." In 3:12, then, Paul can be understood as saying that he who does *all things written in the book of the law* (αὐτα) will live. Here again in Gal 3:12 Paul does not restrict the doer of the law (ὁ ποιήσας) to Jews. We have already seen in Rom 2:13–14 that Paul includes not only Jews but also gentiles in the category of doers of the law (οἱ ποιηταὶ νόμου, Rom 2:13). For Paul, gentiles not having the law can do the law by nature. Lawless gentiles have the Mosaic law since they are the law to themselves (Rom 2:14). As in Rom 2:13–14, Paul in Gal 3:10–13 states Jews' and gentiles' possibility of doing the law by using ὅσοι, πᾶς, οὐδεὶς and the impossibility of their being justified by doing the law as his use of οὐδεὶς indicates ("no one [οὐδεὶς] is justified by the Law before God," Gal 3:11).

By using ὅσοι, πᾶς, οὐδεὶς without restricting to Jews and also by using "he who does them" without limiting to Jews, Paul includes all human beings in his discussion of being under the curse of the law and not being justified by the law in Gal 3:10–12.

CHRIST REDEEMED "US" FROM THE CURSE: GAL 3:13–14

In Gal 3:13, Paul proclaims, "Christ redeemed *us* (ἡμᾶς) from the curse of the law, having become a curse for *us*" (ἡμῶν). Who is the "us" here? Whom did Christ redeem from the curse of the law by his death on the cross? Does "us" mean only Jewish people or all human beings including Paul and Galatian gentiles? The identity of the first person plural pronouns ἡμᾶς and ἡμῶν in this verse has been a subject of debate.

24. Young, "Pronominal Shifts in Paul's Argument to the Galatians," in *Ancient History in a Modern University*, 211.

25. Kim, *Paul and the New Perspective*, 148.

26. Bruce, *Epistle to the Galatians*, 162.

Who Are Redeemed from the Curse of the Law?

Many scholars insist that the first person plural pronouns (ἡμᾶς, ἡμῶν) in Gal 3:13 mean Jews exclusively (exclusive sense of "us"). This view is supported by J. B. Lightfoot, E. W. Burton, Nils Alstrup Dahl, H. D. Betz, Richard B. Hays, T. L. Donaldson, N. T. Wright, Frank J. Matera and others.[27] However, it is more natural to think that Paul includes Galatian gentiles in "us," proclaiming that Christ redeemed gentiles as well as Jews from the curse of the law (inclusive sense of "us"). This view is supported by F. F. Bruce, N. H. Young, Peter Chidolue Onwuka, and many others.[28]

Christ Redeemed Gentiles as Well as Jews

H. D. Betz contends that ἡμᾶς and ἡμῶν in Gal 3:13 refer to Jewish Christians.[29] The reason he provides is that this verse refers back to 2:15, where Paul says "we are Jews by nature (ἡμεῖς φύσει Ἰουδαῖοι) and not sinners from among the gentiles."[30] This interpretation, however, needs to be reconsidered because vocative Ὦ ἀνόητοι Γαλάται in Gal 3:1 marks the shift of Paul's conversation partner from Cephas to gentile Galatians.[31] Thus, the first person pronouns in 3:13 mean Paul the Jew and the gentile Galatians, whereas "we" in 2:15 are Paul and Cephas, namely, Jewish people. Further, while in the case of 2:15, the phrase εἶπον τῷ Κηφᾷ in 2:14 indicates that

27. Dahl, *Studies in Paul*, 132–34; Betz, *Galatians*, 148n101; Hays, *Letter to the Galatians*, 261–62; Hays, *Faith of Jesus Christ*, 102–11; Donaldson, "'Curse of the Law' and the Inclusion of the Gentiles," 95–98; Burton, *Critical and Exegetical Commentary on the Epistle to the Galatians*, 169; Robinson, "Distinction between Jewish and Gentile Believers in Galatians," 34–35; Braswell, "Blessing of Abraham versus 'the Curse of the Law'" 74, 79; Matera, *Galatians*, 120, 124; Boers, *Justification of the Gentiles*, 69; McKnight, *Galatians*, 156; Hong, "Being 'Under the Law' in Galatians," 362; Witherington, *Grace in Galatia*, 236.

28. Ridderbos, *Epistle of Paul to the Churches of Galatia*, 125–26; Young, "Pronominal Shift in Paul's Argument to the Galatians," 210–15; Bruce, *Epistle to the Galatians*, 167; Oepke, *Der Brief des Paulus an die Galater*, 107; Rohde, *Der Brief des Paulus an die Galater*, 145; Hansen, *Abraham in Galatians*, 123; Martyn, *Galatians*, 317–18; Young, "Who's Cursed—and Why?" 90; Wisdom, *Blessing for the Nations and the Curse of the Law*, 191; Tolmie, *Persuading the Galatians*, 121; Onwuka, *Law, Redemption and Freedom in Christ*, 96; Schreiner, *Galatians*, 215; de Boer, *Galatians*, 209; Moo, *Galatians*, 213; Das, *Galatians*, 330–31; DeSilva, *Letter to the Galatians*, 300; Harmon, *Galatians*, 159

29. Betz, *Galatians*, 148.

30. Betz, *Galatians*, 148n101.

31. Similarly DeSilva points out that Paul addresses Galatians as a "you" (pl.) in 3:1–5 as forming "we" to be Paul and Galatians. DeSilva, *Letter to the Galatians*, 300.

the dialogue in 2:15 was performed between Paul and Peter, i.e., the Jewish people; in the case of 3:13, there is no such indication. If there is no clear indication that Paul means Jews exclusively with "we/us," it is natural to think that Paul includes gentile Galatians when he says "we/us" in his letter addressed to them.

As seen already, Paul's use of ὅσοι, πᾶς, οὐδείς, and "he who does them" rather than "Jews" signifies that Paul includes gentiles as well as Jews in the first person plural pronoun in Gal 3:13. N. T. Wright insists that Paul is not concerned with individual sins but corporate sins of Israel, stating, "his point is not that individual Jews have all in fact sinned, but that Israel as a whole has failed to keep the perfect Torah."[32] Using italics, he emphasizes that Gal 3:10 should be interpreted in terms of Israel's national failure to keep the Mosaic law:

> What is envisaged, in other words, is not so much the question
> of what happens *when this or that individual sins*, but the ques-
> tion of what happens when *the nation as a whole fails* to keep *the
> Torah as a whole*.[33]

Wright's interpretation of Gal 3:10–13 is subject to question, since he does not consider the individual sense of ὅσοι, πᾶς, οὐδείς and "he who does them." In Gal 3:13, Paul proclaims that Christ redeemed individual gentiles as well as individual Jews who are under the curse of the law because of their individual sins.

The context of Paul's argument in Gal 3:1–14 proves that gentiles are included in the "we" and redeemed from the curse of the law. Beginning in 3:1 and relying on the Galatians' experience of receiving the Spirit (v. 2, v. 14) and God's miracles working among them (v. 5), Paul argues that no one is justified before God by observing the law (v. 11). No one can keep the law in totality. Abraham was justified by his faith. Failing in complete observance of the law incurs the curse of the law (3:10). Galatian gentile Christians also had been under the curse of the law prior to their believing in Christ due to their falling short of complete obedience to the law. Christ was cursed for Galatians to redeem them from the curse of the law (v. 13). What Christ has done for Galatians is applicable to them "in Christ" (ἐν Χριστῷ Ἰησοῦ, v. 14) and "by/through faith" (ἐκ πίστεως, v.8; διὰ τῆς πίστεως, v. 14) alone. The Galatian Christians' experience of receiving the Spirit and the working power of God among them prove that they have crossed over from the curse

---

32. Wright, *Climax of the Covenant*, 146.

33. Wright, *Climax of the Covenant*, 146. Italics original.

of the law to the blessing of Abraham by faith in Christ rather than by the observance of the law.[34]

Not Gentiles but "Israel as a Whole"

For Wright, the curse of the law is Israel's national plight rather than the individual Jew's plight due to his individual sins. The curse is Israel's problem rather than the gentiles' problem. Therefore, when Paul states in Gal 3:13 that "Christ redeemed us from the curse of the law, by becoming a curse for us," Paul, according to Wright, must have declared that Christ redeemed "Israel as a whole" from the curse of the law by becoming a curse for "Israel as a whole." This interpretation cannot allow ἡμᾶς and ἡμῶν ("us") in Gal 3:13 to be viewed as all human beings including gentile Galatians.

Gentiles Are Not under Torah

According to Wright, gentiles cannot be redeemed from the curse of the law since they are not under the law. Thus, for him, "us" in Gal 3:13 and "we" in Gal 3:14 mean Jews.[35] Wright states:

> It is Jews who are under Torah; Gentiles are only in that state by a peculiar sort of extension, which is only seen (in my judgment) in Colossians 2.14f., which is itself not such an easy passage as to provide a basis for the exegesis of Galatians or Romans. (When Paul aligns the plights of Jews and of Gentiles in 4.1–11, he does not say that Gentiles were under the Torah, but that Jews were under the στοιχεῖα. This has implications for his view of Torah, to be sure, but it cannot mean that the Gentiles were 'under' a law they never possessed.)[36]

For Wright, it is Jews who possessed the law and consequently they needed to be redeemed from its curse. According to Wright, Paul cannot place gentiles under the law.

Ridderbos refers to Rom 2:14 and 15 to say that Jews are not the only ones who live under the law.[37] In Gal 3:13, Paul proclaims that Christ redeemed gentiles as well as Jews ("us") from the curse of the law. It can be observed that Paul places all human beings under the law.

34. Cf. John 5:25.

35. Wright, *Climax of the Covenant*, 143.

36. Wright, *Climax of the Covenant*, 143.

37. Ridderbos, *Epistle of Paul to the Churches of Galatia*, 126n8.

It is not impossible to think that Paul places lawless gentiles under the law. As the second chapter of this book shows, Hellenistic Judaism tended to place gentiles under the Mosaic law. The Mosaic law functions as the criterion for the gentile judgment on God's judgment day. Hellenistic Jews attest to the Mosaic law's universal validity. God the provider of the Mosaic law is the one God who created the world and will judge all human beings. The Mosaic law's universal validity is expressed by various methods in Hellenistic Judaism including identifying universal wisdom with the Mosaic law as seen particularly in Sirach. Even Abraham and other patriarchs who lived before the coming of the Mosaic law were believed to have obeyed the law (Sir 44:20; Philo's *Abr.* 275). Similarly, Paul might have used the Mosaic law as a universal moral norm to prove gentiles' moral failure and their being under the curse. In the light of Hellenistic Judaism, Paul's placing lawless gentiles under the law is, therefore, not an unthinkable idea.

Christ Redeemed Us from the Curse of the Law

Those who are redeemed from the curse of the law in Gal 3:13 are not only Jews but also gentiles. Christ redeemed both Jews and gentiles from the curse of the law. Paul emphasizes Christ as the one who redeemed us from the curse by placing the term at the first part of the sentence.[38] Since Paul states that Jews and gentiles are redeemed from the curse of the law, it follows that Paul understands Jews and gentiles to be under the curse of the law. Without previously being under the curse of the law, one cannot be redeemed from it. For Paul, all human beings are under the curse of the law and Christ is the only one who can redeem them.[39]

Frank J. Matera understands Paul to be referring by "us" to "Jewish believers who have lived under the curse of the Law."[40] However, Paul refers to gentiles as well as Jews by "us," considering all of them to be under the curse of the law. Matera, supporting T. L. Donaldson, notes, "The redemption of the Jews precedes that of the Gentiles."[41] Paul, however, does not

38. Cf. Ridderbos, *Epistle of Paul to the Churches of Galatia*, 125.

39. Christ is proclaimed by the apostles as the only name by which human beings can be saved. Peter boldly proclaims in Acts 4:12, "There is salvation in no one else; for there is no other name under heaven that has been given among men, by which we must be saved." The words "under heaven" (ὑπὸ τὸν οὐρανὸν) and "among men" (ἐν ἀνθρώποις) indicate the salvation Christ provides is intended not only for Jews but also for all human beings.

40. Matera, *Galatians*, 120.

41. Matera, *Galatians*, 120; Donaldson, "The 'Curse of the Law' and the Inclusion of the Gentiles," 94–112.

teach that there are two stages in Christ's redemption of human beings: the first stage for Jews, the second stage for gentiles. Christ's redemptive death on the cross has an immediate saving effect, without partiality, on gentiles as well as Jews who believe in Christ. Paul does not claim that Jews need to be redeemed first by Christ's crucifixion, and gentiles will be saved later, after Jews have been redeemed. Paul clearly proclaims to Galatian gentiles, "Christ redeemed *us* from the curse of the law" by his death on the cross.

The curse from which gentiles as well as Jews are redeemed is the curse of the law (ἐκ τῆς κατάρας τοῦ νόμου). The genitive νόμου is a subjective genitive; thus, the curse of the law means "the curse pronounced by the law."[42] The curse cannot mean the exile of Israel, because Paul places all human beings, Jews and gentiles, under the curse of the law. Many scholars understand the curse of the law to be Israel's particular plight from which Christ needs to redeem her.[43] However, for Paul, being under the curse of the law is the plight of all human beings. Christ redeems gentiles as well as Jews from the same plight, which is the curse of the law.

Paul does not identify the curse of the law as Israel's exile in Gal 3:10–14. Rather, Paul connects the curse of the law to the "death" of individual law breakers. What Paul has in mind is a "life" or "death" issue. Being under the curse of the law means "death." In Gal 3:11, when Paul contends that no man is justified before God by the law, which means that those who are of the works of the law are under the curse of the law, he identifies what the works of the law cannot provide as "life": "The righteous man shall *live* (ζήσεται) by faith." In Gal 3:12, Paul again mentions "life" regarding the law. The only way to live under the law is to do all things written in the book of the law. Thus, Paul states, quoting the Old Testament, "He who does them (ποιήσας αὐτὰ) will *live* (ζήσεται) by them." Then, what would be the result for those who do not do them, i.e, all things written in the book of the law? The result would be "death," the opposite of "life." Galatians 3:10 clearly shows this point. Paul reminds Galatian gentiles that "Cursed is everyone who *does not* abide by all things written in the book of the law, to *do* them (ποιῆσαι αὐτα,)." If those who keep the law live and those who do not keep it are under the curse of the law, the curse of the law implies the death of the law breakers. In Gal 3:13, the curse of the law Christ bears for "us" is death on the cross. Even in Gal 3:21, law is mentioned with regard to life and death: "If a law had been given which was able to impart life (ζωοποιῆσαι), then righteousness would indeed have been based on law." This verse implies two things: first, the law

42. Hong, *Law in Galatians*, 79.

43. Donaldson, "The 'Curse of the Law' and the Inclusion of the Gentiles," 98, 102–105; Hong, *Law in Galatians*, 84.

cannot provide life but pronounces death to those who are under it; second, righteousness, which is tantamount to life in this verse, is not based on law. In Rom 1:32, Paul accuses those who do the evil things he just enumerated in the previous verses, because "they know God's decree (τὸ δικαίωμα) that those who do such things deserve to *die* (θανάτου)." The wages of sin is *death* and sin is reckoned by the law (Rom 5:13, 6:23). In this regard, Ridderbos is right in his understanding of those who are under the curse as "persons appointed to die."[44] Leon Morris similarly states, "The curse meant a death sentence and sinners are ransomed from this by the death of Jesus."[45] Death "refers to both spiritual death—separation from God—and physical death."[46]

Christ Became a Curse for Us

All human beings were subject to death because of their being under the curse of the law due to their inability to keep the whole law. Christ's death on the cross is his vicarious death for us. Thus, Paul states in Gal 3:13 that Christ became a curse for us (ὑπὲρ ἡμῶν).[47] Redeeming us from the curse of the law means providing life to us. Righteousness, which cannot be obtained by the law, means life in Gal 3:21. In Romans, the law from which those who are in Christ are set free is "the law of sin and of *death*" (νόμου τῆς ἁμαρτίας καὶ τοῦ θανάτου [Rom 8:2]). Ridderbos is, thus, correct in his statement, "It is from this sentence of death that Christ had redeemed them by Himself 'becoming a curse' for them—that is to say, a cursed one."[48] In Paul's presentation of his gospel, the curse of the law is not explained in terms of exile. Paul does not claim that Christ's death on the cross means his death for Israel to make her return from exile.

44. Ridderbos, *Epistle of Paul to the Churches of Galatia*, 127.

45. Morris, *Galatians*, 106.

46. Schreiner, *New Testament Theology*, 534. Schreiner interprets "death" in Rom 5:21 as both spiritual death and physical death. The same interpretation can be applied to Galatians. Christ, who bore our curse by the death on the cross, experienced not only our physical death but also our separation from God (spiritual death) as his crying out shows, "'Eli, Eli, lama sabachthani?' that is, 'My God, My God, why have you forsaken me?'" Because of Christ's death on the cross for us, "we"—Jews and Gentiles—now experience the sonship of God in Christ ("You are all sons of God through faith in Christ Jesus" [Gal 3:26]) and expect the bodily resurrection (1 Cor 15:52).

47. The thought of substitution can be found in the words "for us" (ὑπὲρ ἡμῶν). Christ's curse was not his own curse but our curse. He bore our curse in our place. Paul's use of ὑπὲρ ἡμῶν in 2 Cor 5:21 also shows the sense of substitution. God made Christ who knew no sin to be sin for us (ὑπὲρ ἡμῶν), that we might become the righteousness of God in him (2 Cor 5:21). For the thought of substitution in Gal 3:13, see Morris, *Galatians*, 106.

48. Ridderbos, *Epistle of Paul to the Churches of Galatia*, 127.

The curse of the law and the redemption from the curse should not be understood in a sociological perspective. The curse of the law is the death of individual law breakers and Christ died for them to provide a new life in him. Paul indeed confesses that his union with Christ in crucifixion means his death and Christ's new life in him (Gal 2:20).

Blessing of Abraham and Gentiles in Christ

With two ἵνα clauses, Paul expresses in Gal 3:14 the purpose of Christ's redemption of "us" from the curse of the law.[49] The first purpose is to make the blessing of Abraham available to gentiles in Christ Jesus (ἐν Χριστῷ Ἰησου). Gentiles cannot be the recipient of Abraham's blessing by law observance. The blessing of Abraham is available for gentiles only in Christ, because Christ died for them on the cross.

Galatians 3:14 and Gentiles under the Law

The "we" in λάβωμεν in Gal 3:14 supports the inclusive reading of "us" in Gal 3:13. Paul states in 3:14 that "*we* might receive (λάβωμεν) the promise of the Spirit through faith." The pronoun "we" in this verse includes the Galatians, since Galatian gentile Christians are described as having received the Spirit in Gal 3:2 and 5.[50] It is more natural, then, to think that Paul refers to the same group by "us/we" in two adjoining verses, i.e., Gal 3:13 and 14 rather than to think that he refers to "the Jews" in 3:13, and to "Jews and gentiles" in 3:14. Consequently, Paul puts gentiles under the law and its curse in Gal 3:13.

Christ's Crucifixion: Gal 3:1 and 3:14

Christ's crucifixion is the reason why Galatian gentiles should not be bewitched by Judaisers (Gal 3:1). For Paul, Christ's crucifixion is directly related to gentiles. Christ was publically portrayed as crucified before the eyes of Galatian gentiles. Christ's crucifixion has a significant meaning for them. Therefore, if they are bewitched without understanding the meaning of Christ's crucifixion, they are "foolish Galatians." This direct relationship between Christ's crucifixion and gentile Galatians is reaffirmed in Gal 3:13 when Paul uses "us" regarding the beneficiary of Christ's death on the cross. The meaning of Christ's crucifixion for gentile Galatians is their redemption

49. Bruce, *Epistle to the Galatians*, 167.

50. Martyn, *Galatians*, 323, 335.

from the curse of the law. It should not be overlooked that Paul's mention of Christ's crucifixion in Gal 3:1 and 3:14 is aimed at gentile Galatians. In Gal 3:14, crucifixion is interpreted in relation to gentiles. Because of Christ's crucifixion, Abraham's blessing comes to gentiles, and "we," gentiles as well as Jews, receive the Holy Spirit. After all, in Gal 3:1, 13 and 14, Paul's concern is to remind gentile Galatians of the meaning of Christ's crucifixion, so that they may not be led astray by Judaisers. For Paul, Christ's crucifixion publicly portrayed before the Galatians' eyes means that they are redeemed from the curse of the law and receive Abraham's blessing in Christ by faith.

GENTILES UNDER THE LAW IN GAL 3:23–25

In Gal 3:23–25, Paul places gentiles as well as Jews under the law. He depicts human beings who were imprisoned (συγκλειόμενοι, Gal 3:23) under the law as those living under παιδαγωγός (Gal 3:24). For Paul, before faith came, all human beings, Jews and gentiles, were confined and imprisoned under the law and were living under παιδαγωγός. When Christ and faith came, human beings were liberated from being imprisoned under the law and from being under παιδαγωγός. Now those who are in Christ Jesus are *sons* of God through faith (Gal 3:26). They are no longer under παιδαγωγός. Paul proclaims to Galatian gentile Christians in Gal 3:26, "*You* are all sons of God through faith in Christ Jesus." "You" means Galatian gentile Christians. Gal 3:26 makes it clear that faith and Christ play a crucial role for gentiles to become sons. In Gal 3:25, Paul uses "we" rather than "you" to teach the same message as he proclaims in Gal 3:26: "But now that faith has come, we are no longer under a παιδαγωγός." Faith is the key element to liberate "we" from being under παιδαγωγός. The law functions as παιδαγωγός until Christ comes, so that "we" might be justified by faith.

Paul argues that Christ and faith will finish law's the function as a παιδαγωγός and "we" will become sons of God. Thus, Gal 3:26 is the conclusion of Paul's explanations in Gal 3:23–25, in which Paul uses "we." In Gal 3:26, he directly applies what he explained in previous verses to gentile Galatians by shifting from "we" to "you." The gentile Galatians are now sons of God in Christ through faith. Paul's argument is that when they were without Christ and faith, they were under the law and could not be sons of God because of the function of the law as παιδαγωγός. In Gal 3:29, Paul confirms that gentiles are Abraham's seed (σπέρμα) and heirs according to promise if they belong to Christ. While he uses "Christ" in Gal 3:29, he employs "faith" in Gal 3:7 to show how to be a son of Abraham. For Paul, gentiles as well as Jews become Abraham's seed and heirs, not by works of the law but by faith in Christ.

The reason for understanding that Paul places gentiles under the law in Gal 3:23 can be found in Gal 3:22 as well. Paul points out in Gal 3:22, "The scripture has imprisoned (συνέκλεισεν) all things (τὰ πάντα) under sin." "All things" (τὰ πάντα) which were imprisoned under sin in Gal 3:22 can be understood as all human beings, Jews and gentiles.[51] In the very next verse, that is, in Gal 3:23, Paul replaces "all things" with "we," stating that "we" are confined and imprisoned (συγκλειόμενοι) under the law. Since Paul claims all human beings are imprisoned under sin in Gal 3:22, he is likely referring to all human beings when he claims that "we" are confined and imprisoned under the law in Gal 3:23.

Living under the law requires people to keep all the law to be justified, as Gal 3:10 implies. Before faith and Christ came, all people were sinners because no one could keep the law perfectly. Thus, Paul points out in Gal 3:22, "The scripture has imprisoned (συνέκλεισεν) all things (τὰ πάντα) under sin." There is no one who can keep "all things written in the book of the law" (Gal 3:10) and who is not imprisoned under sin.[52] It is, therefore, a fair judgment to imprison all things under sin. "All things" (τὰ πάντα) were imprisoned under sin and "we" are confined and imprisoned under the law.

In Gal 3:22–23, Paul closely relates "to be under sin" with "to be under the law." Paul seems to say that all who sin are under the law. Gentiles are no exception in being imprisoned under the law given the fact that they are all sinners as well. In addition to Gal 3:22, Paul maintains similarly in Rom 3:9 that gentiles are under sin, proclaiming, "For we have already charged that both Jews and Greeks are all under sin." Gentiles are under the law as long as they are sinners. In his salvation-historical explanation, Paul denotes the temporary nature of the law, namely, "before faith came, we were confined under the law" (Gal 3:23), the "law has become our παιδαγωγός until the time of Christ" (εἰς Χριστόν, Gal 3:24).[53] Before faith and Christ came, "we" are confined under the law, which plays the role of παιδαγωγός for us. Since "we" includes "everyone (τὰ πάντα)" who is under sin according to the parallel construction between verses 22 and 23, "we" in verses 23–25 refers to gentiles as well. As long as gentiles are under sin, they are under the law in Paul's theology. Only when Christ comes and gentiles believe in him can gentile sinners be released from παιδαγωγός to become sons of God (Gal

51. Dunn, *Epistle to the Galatians*, 194.

52. Bruce understands ἡ γραφὴ in Gal 3:22 to be "the written law", concentrated in such an uncompromising form as Dt. 27:26 (quoted in v 10 above)." Bruce, *Epistle to the Galatians*, 180.

53. For the temporal rendering of εἰς, see Schreiner, *Law and Its Fulfillment*, 128.

3:26). For Paul, gentiles are always under the law before they unite with Christ by faith (Gal 3:26–27).

In this context, the law as παιδαγωγός is not likely used as an educator or restrainer of sin. Seifrid detects three aspects of παιδαγωγός's function here: (1) depriving people of freedom, (2) identifying the people under παιδαγωγός as ones in the status of minors, (3) temporary role of παιδαγωγός.[54] As Seifrid points out, the effect of the law is to imprison all things under sin.[55] Gentiles as well as Jews were imprisoned under sin when they were under the law because they could not keep the whole law. They were under the curse of the law (Gal 3:10, 13). But this period was temporary. God sent forth Christ and whoever believes in him is no longer under παιδαγωγός but becomes a son of God.

In Gal 3:24, Paul contrasts justification by faith and the law's function as παιδαγωγός. In Galatians chapter 3, justification by faith is what Paul emphasizes as the general way of salvation for Jews and gentiles. Thus, "we" who are justified by faith in Gal 3:24 are likely Jews and gentiles. If Paul makes a parallel between justification of all human beings by faith and the law's function as παιδαγωγός in the context where Paul points out human beings' inability to keep the whole law and then provides faith in Christ as the alternate way of salvation for human beings, then the law functioning as παιδαγωγός can be applied to all human beings.

GALATIANS 4:3–6 AND GENTILES

In Gal 4:5, Paul states that Christ came to redeem those who were under the law, so that we might receive the adoption as sons. Whom does Paul have in mind when he proclaims that Christ came to redeem those who were under the law (τοὺς ὑπὸ νόμον)? Does he mean that Christ came to redeem only Jews in this verse, since they are the only people who are under the law? Or, does he claim that Christ came to redeem gentiles as well as Jews by including all of them in the category of those who are under the law? Who are "we" in this verse? Does Paul refer to either gentiles or Jews, or both Jews and gentiles when he states, "We might receive the adoption as sons"?

Hays sees "we" in this verse as the gentiles, while "us" in Gal 3:13 as the Jews.[56] According to Hays, Paul stated in Gal 3:13 that Christ redeemed

54. Seifrid, *Christ, Our Righteousness*, 108n52; According to John B. Polhill, παιδαγωγός were "household slaves who served as custodians of children between the ages of six and sixteen." Polhill, *Paul and His Letters*, 149.

55. Seifrid, *Christ, Our Righteousness*, 108n51.

56. Hays, *Faith of Jesus Christ*, 107.

Jews ("us") from the curse of the law (cf. Gal 4:5a) and then states in Gal 4:5b that gentiles ("we") receive the adoption as sons. For Hays, this interpretation can be used as the evidence for Paul's use of traditional formulations or the evidence for his use of rhetoric to identify himself with two different people groups, i.e., Jews or gentiles.[57] According to the view of Paul's use of traditional formulations in Gal 4:5 Paul might have cited a traditional formulation from gentile-Christian communities ("us" = gentiles). In contrast, in Gal 3:13 he might have cited a traditional formulation from Jewish-Christian communities ("we" = Jews).[58] Hence, Hays supposes that "Paul for rhetorical purposes alternately identifies himself with these two different constituencies."[59] Reference is made to 1 Cor 9:20–21 to bolster this supposition, where Paul confesses that he can identify himself with various kinds of people to win them. Hays, however, confesses that "it is impossible to decide between these two possibilities on the basis of narrative structure alone."[60] Nevertheless, he concludes regarding "us" in Gal 3:13 and "we" in 4:5, "We can only say that one formulation tells the story from a Gentile point of view and that the other tells it from a Jewish point of view."[61]

Although Hays' interpretation is interesting, there are some questions that must be resolved. Does Paul speak from the Jewish perspective and from the gentile perspective in Gal 3:13 and Gal 4:5 respectively? And how can it be proved? Could Paul have referred to two different groups with the same first person plural without any clear indication for doing so? Is it not more natural to think that Paul refers to the same people group, either Jews or gentiles, or both Jews and gentiles by "we"/"us" in Gal 3:13 and 4:5? Furthermore, the argument based on the hypothesis of traditional formulations from gentile-Christian communities or from Jewish-Christian communities is hard to prove. It is only a hypothesis and therefore subject to debate.

Paul does not indicate either in Gal 3:13 or in Gal 4:5 that he is speaking from a certain perspective or that he is shifting from one perspective to another. Therefore, it is more reasonable to think that Paul uses "we" and "us" in a consistent manner to refer to the same people group. If Hays identifies "we" in Gal 4:5 as gentiles, "us" in Gal 3:13 also needs to be understood as gentiles. Or if he sees "us" in Gal 3:13 as Jews, "we" in Gal 4:5 also needs to refer to Jews. However, he believes that Paul refers to Jews by "us" in Gal 3:13, whereas Paul means gentiles by "we" in Gal 4:5.

---

57. Hays, *Faith of Jesus Christ*, 107–108.

58. Hays, *Faith of Jesus Christ*, 107.

59. Hays, *Faith of Jesus Christ*, 107.

60. Hays, *Faith of Jesus Christ*, 108.

61. Hays, *Faith of Jesus Christ*, 108.

There is another issue to be solved regarding Hays' interpretation of Gal 4:5. Hays understands "we" in this verse to be referring only to gentiles. However, it is more natural to understand that Paul is referring to both Galatians (gentiles) and himself (Jews) by "we" in this verse. It is clear that when Paul refers to Galatians alone he uses "you" rather than "we" in the very next verse (ὅτι δέ ἐστε υἱοί, "because you are sons," Gal 4:6a). In Gal 4:6b Paul returns to "we" from "you" when he says, "God has sent forth the Spirit of his Son into our hearts (καρδίας ἡμῶν), crying, 'Abba! Father!'" Regarding Gal 4:6b, however, Hays acknowledges that Paul refers to Jews and gentiles by "we." For Hays, whereas "we" who receive the adoption as sons in Gal 4:5 are only gentiles, "we" who have the Spirit of God's Son in Gal 4:6 are Jews and gentiles. One may wonder if this inconsistent interpretation of "we" in Gal 4:5 and 6 is legitimate. If "we" in Gal 4:6 is understood to be both Jews and gentiles, "we" in Gal 4:5 needs to be understood as both Jews and gentiles as well.

Thus, Hays interpretation of Gal 4:5 and 4:6 regarding "we" and "you" is as follows:[62]

4:5a	Christ redeemed those who were under the law	(= Jews)
4:5b	so that "we" might receive the adoption as sons	(we = gentiles)
4:6a	because "you" are sons	(you = gentiles)
4:6b	the Spirit of God's Son has been sent into "our" hearts	(we = Jews and gentiles)

Galatians 4:5 and 4:6, however, can be better understood when we interpret them as follows:

4:5a	Christ redeemed those who were under the law	(= Jews and gentiles)
4:5b	"we" receive the adoption as sons	("we" = Jews and gentiles)
4:6a	because "you" are sons	("you" = gentiles)
4:6b	the Spirit of God's Son has been sent into "our" hearts	(we = Jews and gentiles)

In this interpretation, those who are redeemed are both Jews and gentiles. "Us" in Gal 3:13 ("Christ redeemed us") are both Jews and gentiles. Therefore, those who are under the law but redeemed by Christ in Gal 4:5a

---

62. Hays, *Faith of Jesus Christ*, 95–101, 107.

are both Jews and gentiles.[63] "We" in Gal 4:5b and 4:6b are Jews and gentiles. Ronald Fung is correct in his interpretation of "we" in Gal 4:3–5 as both Jews and gentiles. When he interprets "we" in Gal 4:3, he states as follows:

> The emphatic "we" here (*hēmeis*, NEB "us"), like the first person plural in 3:13f., probably embraces both Jews and Gentiles, since the transition from "we might attain the status of sons" (v. 5) to "because you are sons" (v. 6, RSV) suggests that the "we" of vv. 3–5 includes the "you," the Galatians converts of Gentile origin.[64]

"Born under the Law" in Gal 4:4

Many scholars conclude that being "born under the law" means that Christ was a Jewish man.[65] Regarding the phrase "born under the law," Dunn notes, "Here, of course, the Jewishness of Jesus, and indeed his practice as a devout Jew, is emphasized."[66] George similarly comments on this phrase, "He also was a Jewish man, circumcised on the eighth day as all Jewish males were. He grew up in a Jewish home reading the Torah, praying to his Heavenly Father, attending synagogue."[67] The phrase "born under the law" may have been used in Judaism as a designation for a person's being a Jew. However, this information or observation does not automatically warrant that whenever Paul uses this phrase, he always means someone's being a Jew. Of course, Jesus' being born under the law fits with Jesus' being a Jew, since Jews were under the Mosaic law, and nobody denies Jesus was a Jew. Nevertheless, Paul's use of this expression in Gal 4:4 should not be understood as his reference to Christ's merely being a Jewish man. As Hellenistic Jews recognize the Mosaic law's universal validity and, therefore, place even gentiles under the judgment of the Mosaic law, Paul understands that gentiles have the law as well. As our investigation of Romans in chapter 2 indicates, in Paul's mind lawless gentiles hear the law speaking to them and are under the judgment of God and equally with Jews are without excuse. Christ's birth under the law can be understood as his becoming a human being in addition to becoming a Jew. Although the Jews received the written

---

63. So also, Oakes, 134.

64. Fung, *Epistle to the Galatians*, 181.

65. Betz, *Galatians*, 207; Longenecker, *Galatians*, 171; Hansen, *Galatians*, 118; Hays, *Letter to the Galatians*, 283; George, *Galatians*, 303; Williams, *Galatians*, 111; Rosner, *Paul and the Law*, 49 ("by which Paul simply means that Jesus was a Jew").

66. Dunn, *Epistle to the Galatians*, 216.

67. George, *Galatians*, 303.

law of Moses, they are not the only people who are under the law in Paul's theological argument. Christ needs to be born under the law to redeem all human beings who are under the law.

If Paul refers to Christ's being Jewish man by the phrase "born under the law" in Gal 4:4, the purpose of Christ's incarnation Paul describes in Gal 4:5 must be understood as follows: Christ became a Jewish man ("born under the law") to redeem only Jewish people ("those who were under the law"). However, Paul is not likely to claim that Christ became a Jew to redeem only Jewish people with the expressions "born under the law" and "redeem those who were under the law." Rather, Paul refers to Christ's becoming a human being by the words "born under the law" and refers to Christ's redemption of all human beings by the phrase "to redeem those who were under the law." In Gal 4:4–5, Paul places all human beings under the law when he explains Christ's incarnation and redemption. Christ became under the law to redeem all human beings from the curse of the law (Gal 4:4, 5; Gal 3:13).

It is helpful to consider the expression "born of a woman" to understand "born under the law." Scholars generally agree that the expression "born of a woman" does not refer to Christ's virgin birth.[68] Bruce comments regarding this expression, "It throws no light on the question whether he knew of Jesus' virginal conception or not."[69] Scholars understand that "born of a woman" is used to portray Christ's status as a human being.[70] Referring to Job 14:1 and Matt 11:11, Martyn comments, "The expression means to be born as a human being."[71] In addition, Longenecker notes, "'born of a woman' speaks of Jesus' true humanity and representative quality—i.e., that he was truly one with us, who came as "the Man" to stand in our place."[72] The reason why Paul might have not meant the virginal conception of Christ by "born of a woman" Fung states as follows:

> In any case, it is perhaps unlikely that Paul does have the virginal conception in view here, for the context lays emphasis on the identification of the Son of God with those he came to redeem;

---

68. Fung, *Epistle to the Galatians*, 182; Longenecker, *Galatians*, 171; Dunn, *Epistle to the Galatians*, 215.

69. Bruce, *Epistle to the Galatians*, 195.

70. Dunn, *Epistle to the Galatians*, 215; George, *Galatians*, 302; Although Paul might have not referred to Christ's virginal conception by "born of a woman" in this verse, as Timothy George contends, "it is inconceivable that Paul, the travel companion of Luke, would not have known about the virginal conception of Jesus." See George, *Galatians*, 302.

71. Martyn, *Galatians*, 390.

72. Longenecker, *Galatians*, 171.

'hence he is stressing the likeness to us in terms of birth rather than the distinction from us in terms of conception.'"[73]

Just as Paul means Christ's becoming a human being by "born of a woman," so he, by "born under the law," seems to refer to Christ's being born as a human being rather than merely as a Jew. "Born under the law" signifies Christ's being born in the likeness of men as a true representative of human beings. When Paul mentions Jesus' incarnation in Phil 2:7, he points out the fact that Jesus was "born in the likeness of men." Although Jesus was "in the form of God" (Phil 2:6), he "emptied himself" by taking the form of a slave and by taking on the likeness of man.[74] Christ's incarnation means Christ's becoming a perfect man without giving up his divinity. For Longenecker, "born of a woman" refers to Christ's true humanity and representative quality, but "born under the law" simply refers to Christ's being a Jew.[75] However, it seems more likely that Paul emphasizes Christ's true humanity and representative quality by those two expressions. By being "born under the law," Jesus Christ became like human beings in terms of their being under the law to bear their curse of the law. Christ's being born under the law reminds us of Heb 4:15, which says that Christ is the "one who has been tempted in all things as we are, yet without sin." Christ became like human beings by being born under the law. He is, however, unlike human beings in that he is not under sin. In 2 Cor 5:21, Paul states that God made Christ "who did not know sin to be sin for us, so that we might become the righteousness of God in him." Likewise, Paul states in Gal 3:13, 4:3 and 4:4 that Christ was born under the law and became a curse for us, so that we might receive the adoption as sons. Christ could be a curse for us because he was not under sin although he was under the law as the representative of all human beings. In Paul's mind, all human beings are under the law and under obligation to keep it perfectly to be justified before God. However, no one can keep the law perfectly.

In addition, when we compare Gal 4:3 with 4:4, we discover that being "born under the law" means becoming a human being. In Gal 4:3 human beings are described as those who are "ὑπὸ τὰ στοιχεῖα τοῦ κόσμου" in their childhood. In order to liberate human beings from being "ὑπὸ τὰ στοιχεῖα τοῦ κόσμου," God sent forth his Son when the fullness of the time came (Gal 4:4). What is intriguing is that Paul says that Christ was born under the

73. Fung, *Epistle to the Galatians*, 182.

74. For a more detailed discussion on the characteristics of Jesus' incarnation in Phil 2:6–7, see Kim, "Imitating Christ: An Exegetical Study of Philippians 2:5–11," *Adorare Mente*, 2–13.

75. Longenecker, *Galatians*, 171–72.

law. Paul employs in Gal 4:4 the words ὑπὸ νόμον instead of ὑπὸ τὰ στοιχεῖα τοῦ κόσμου (Gal 4:3). Paul seems to use ὑπὸ νόμον as tantamount to ὑπὸ τὰ στοιχεῖα τοῦ κόσμου. Christ's being born under the law is to become like human beings who are ὑπὸ τὰ στοιχεῖα τοῦ κόσμου. In Gal 4:5, Paul declares that Christ redeems those who are ὑπὸ νόμον. Those who are ὑπὸ νόμον in Gal 4:5 are those who are ὑπὸ τὰ στοιχεῖα τοῦ κόσμου in Gal 4:3.

Gentiles under the Law in Gal 4:4–5

Although Richard N. Longenecker finds in these verses "a pre-Pauline confessional portion drawn from the proclamation of the early church,"[76] it does not hinder us from investigating Paul's understanding of Christ's person and work and the purpose of God's sending his son in these verses. Whether or not the confession was original with Paul, it is evident that Paul approves the content as if it were his own by including it in his letter.

In Gal 4:4–5, Christ is confessed to have been sent (1) to redeem those who were under the law (ἵνα τοὺς ὑπὸ νόμον ἐξαγοράσῃ, v.5a) and (2) so that *we* might receive sonship (ἵνα τὴν υἱοθεσίαν ἀπολάβωμεν, v.5b). The parallel ἵνα clauses seem to denote that "those who have been redeemed by Christ are the 'we' who through him receives its instatement as sons."[77] The following are some grounds for viewing that Paul places gentiles under the law in Gal 4:5:

1. The parallel ἵνα clauses are likely connecting those who were under the Law and redeemed by Christ with the first person pronoun "we," as we have seen above.

2. Paul's use of a parallel construction between 5b and 6a using the word "sonship/son" indicates that Paul has the Galatians in mind by his use of "we" in 5b.

   5b: so that *we* might receive *sonship* (ἵνα τὴν υἱοθεσίαν ἀπολάβωμεν, v.5b)
   6a: Because *you* are *sons* (Ὅτι δέ ἐστε υἱοί, 6a)

   Since Paul has the Galatians in view in referring to those who were redeemed from the curse of the law and received sonship in Gal 4:5, he switches from *we* to *you* (Galatians) without any intermediate explanation for doing so. "We" (Jews and gentiles) are redeemed and accepted as sons before God by Christ's coming and dying in the likeness of human beings ("born of a woman," "born under the law," Gal 4:4) on the cross (Gal 3:13).

76. Longenecker, *Galatians*, 167.

77. Bruce, *Epistle to the Galatians*, 197.

3. Being under the στοιχεῖα (Gal 4:3) is used interchangeably with being under the law in Gal 4:3 and 5. Those who were under the στοιχεῖα (Gal 3:3) are "we" who were also under the law (Gal 3:5). As J. Louis Martyn comments, all human beings are under the στοιχεῖα and the law.[78] Thus, in Paul's mind, the Galatians' submitting to the law by keeping days and months and seasons and years equals returning to "the weak and poor στοιχεῖα" (4:9–11).[79]

4. The pronominal alternation between "we" and "you" (Galatian gentile Christians) in Gal 4:3–7 means that "we" who are under the στοιχεῖα and the law includes gentiles.[80] In Gal 4:3–7, Paul places all human beings under the law and στοιχεῖα. Gentiles, who do not have the law, are confined under the law, since they are proclaimed by Paul to be under the στοιχεῖα, which is tantamount to the law. Gentiles are held as slaves (δεδουλωμένοι) under the στοιχεῖα (Gal 4:3). Only when Christ comes and redeems those under law will they receive the sonship (υἱοθεσίαν, Gal 4:5). Gentiles are sons of God emancipated from the bondage of the law by the death of Christ. After Paul illustrates in Rom 7:1 that the law rules over a man as long as he lives (ὁ νόμος κυριεύει τοῦ ἀνθρώπου ἐφ᾽ ὅσον χρόνον ζῇ), he proclaims freedom to Roman Christians by saying, "My brothers, you also died to the law through the body of Christ" (ἀδελφοί μου, καὶ ὑμεῖς ἐθανατώθητε τῷ νόμῳ διὰ τοῦ σώματος τοῦ Χριστοῦ). Likewise, in Gal 4:7, Paul proclaims freedom to the Galatian gentile Christians, saying, "therefore you are no longer a slave, but a son." This freedom from bondage was given to gentiles by Christ's death for those under the law (Gal 4:5). Christ died for gentiles to set them free from the bondage of the law and to make them sons of God. This privilege can be given to gentiles only by their union with Christ in his death to the law.

---

78. Martyn, *Galatians*, 334–36; Linda L. Belleville proposes that 4:1–5 refers to Jewish life under law, further arguing that "it is only after establishing the basis of sonship for the Jew in vv. 1–5 that Paul turns to the Gentiles in vv. 6–11 (see the shift from ἦμεν to ἐστε)." However, her argument is unconvincing. Belleville, "Under Law: Structural Analysis and the Pauline Concept of Law in Galatians 3:21–4:11," 68.

79. So also Schreiner. He rightly observes that "Paul forges a connection between 'the elements of the world' and life under the law." Schreiner, *Law and Its Fulfillment*, 80.

80. The most striking alternation appears in Gal 4:6, where Paul says "Because *you* are sons, God sent the Spirit of his Son into *our* hearts." It is evident that Paul includes gentiles in his word "we/us."

"WE," ONLY GENTILES?

Although this book contends that Paul understands gentiles not having the law to be under the law in Galatians, it does not mean that Paul refers to *only Gentiles* by the pronoun "we" in 3:12–14, 3:23–29 and 4:1–5. William J. Dalton, being heavily influenced by Lloyd Gaston, argues that "'we' refers to pagans, not to the Jews."[81] He provides the following reasons: (1) Paul identifies himself with the Galatians, thus "we" means gentiles; (2) There are no Jewish Christians among the Galatians; (3) The term "under the law" applies to "God-fearers" who hoped to find salvation by observing some of the precepts of the law; (4) In Jewish writings, the Jews are never described as people "under the law"; (5) According to Rom 9:4, Paul states that *sonship* belongs to the Israelites. Jews could hardly be regarded as "*slaves* to the elemental spirits of the universe."[82]

Dalton claims that "at least, when Paul uses 'we' in the letter, we are justified in thinking that he is identifying himself with his hearers unless we have good cause for taking another meaning."[83] The burden of proof is on the part of Dalton, however, regarding the cause for taking the meaning of "we" as he does, i.e., that Paul completely absorbs himself into the Galatians and never refers to himself, a Jew, by "we." Martin seems to be more persuasive in his statement that "unless otherwise indicated it would be natural to see 'we' as referring to Paul and his Galatian readers and 'you' as referring to his Galatian readers who are mainly but not exclusively Gentile."[84]

CONCLUSION

In this chapter, we have explored Galatians to see if Paul places gentiles under the law. In Gal 3:13, Paul proclaims that Christ redeemed us from the curse of the law, having become a curse for us. Paul includes gentiles as well as Jews in "us" here. Paul places lawless gentiles under the law and its curse when he explains his gospel to gentiles. Consequently, it can be said that Christ died for Jews and gentiles to redeem them from the curse of the law.

Paul explains Christ's death on the cross as Christ's becoming a curse for all human beings, not just for Jews. Because of Christ's atoning death on the cross, all human beings including gentiles receive the blessing of Abraham in Christ and receive the promise of the Spirit through faith (Gal 3:14).

---

81. Dalton, "Meaning of 'We' in Galatians," 40;

82. Dalton, "Meaning of 'We' in Galatians," 36–40. Emphasis mine.

83. Dalton, "Meaning of 'We' in Galatians," 37.

84. Martin, *Christ and the Law in Paul*, 103.

In Gal 3:23–25, Paul explains that, before faith and Christ came, all human beings were confined and imprisoned under the law. Being under the law means being under παιδαγωγός. By faith in Christ, gentiles as well as Jews become sons of God.

Paul teaches in Gal 4:4–5 that Christ was born under the law to redeem those who were under the law. Although some scholars insist that Paul refers to Christ's being a Jew by the phrase "born under the law" and refers to Christ's redemption of Jewish people by the phrase "to redeem those who were under the law," Paul refers to Christ's becoming a human being and his redemption of human beings by these two expressions. The purpose of Christ's incarnation is to redeem all human beings who are under the law. Because of Christ's redemptive death, Jews and gentiles who are in Christ call God "Abba, Father" (Gal 4:6). It is apparent for Paul that not only Jews but also gentiles need Christ who redeems those under the law from the curse of the law, because all human beings are under the law and its curse. In Paul's mind, lawless gentiles are under the law as well.

As we have seen in chapter 2, Hellenistic Judaism places gentiles under the Mosaic law and its judgment. Hellenistic Jews understand the Mosaic law as universal moral norms. The Mosaic law's universal validity is expressed by various methods including identifying universal wisdom with the Mosaic law and emphasizing God as the creator of the universe. In Galatians, Paul, a Hellenistic Jew, does not explicitly explain how gentiles are under the law. He simply explicates his gospel with the presupposition that gentiles are under the law. Paul explains the meaning of Christ's redemptive death on the cross to Galatian gentile Christians as their redemption from the curse of the law, liberation from παιδαγωγός, receiving the Holy Spirit, and becoming sons of God. According to Hellenistic Judaism, Paul's placing lawless gentiles under the law is not an unthinkable idea. In Galatians, Paul's soteriology can be properly interpreted when we understand that Paul places gentiles as well as Jews under the law and its curse.

CHAPTER 5

Summary and Conclusion

WHAT DOES PAUL SAY about the relationship between the law and gentiles? Paul acknowledges that gentiles do not have the Mosaic law in Rom 2:14. He also acknowledges in Rom 9:4 that the Mosaic law was given to the Jews as their ethnic privilege. It is true that the Mosaic law was given to Israel on Mount Sinai. Are gentiles, then, not under the law in Paul? Many scholars think that only Jews are under the law in Paul. Thus, they understand with regard to Rom 3:19 that the law speaks only to the Jews "who are under the law." Those who are under the curse of the law in Gal 3:10 are only Jews, because they are the only people under the law. Scholars interpret Paul's soteriological statement in Gal 3:13 as relevant only to the Jews: Christ redeemed "us," that is, Jews, from "the curse of the law." In Gal 4:5, Paul states that the purpose of Christ's incarnation is to redeem Jews "who were under the law." Only Jews are under παιδαγωγός and liberated from it by faith in Gal 3:24–25. This understanding, however, fails to apprehend Paul's soteriology for gentiles in full. Paul places gentiles along with Jews under the Mosaic law which they did not receive on Mount Sinai to explain his gospel to gentiles.

The fact that Paul places gentiles who do not have the law under the law perplexes some, such as Heikki Räisänen. Räisänen has started with a correct observation but has reached a wrong conclusion. Räisänen is correct in seeing that Paul puts gentiles under the curse of the law in Gal 3:13 by the first-person plural.[1] Moreover, he is right in observing that Paul distinguishes Jews from gentiles in terms of their possession of the law, that is,

---

1. Räisänen, *Paul and the Law*, 18–23.

Jews live under the law and gentiles are without the law. From these correct observations, however, Räisänen draws an unconvincing conclusion that these are the "pointers to Paul's *personal theological problems*" because of his [Paul's] confusion.[2] He holds that "contradictions and tensions have to be *accepted* as *constant* features of Paul's theology of the law. They are not simply of an accidental or peripheral nature."[3]

However, Paul's placing gentiles under the law is neither his personal theological problem, nor his confusion, nor an unthinkable concept. This book has scrutinized Hellenistic Jewish literature to prove that Paul's placing gentiles under the law has common ground in Hellenistic Judaism. Sirach, Wisdom of Solomon, Baruch, 4 Ezra, 2 Baruch, Philo of Alexandria, Pseudo-Philo's *Biblical Antiquities* witness to Hellenistic Judaism placing gentiles under the law.

In Rom 1:18–32, Paul asserts that, although gentiles did not receive the written form of the Mosaic law, they have the knowledge of God from the creation. They know the will of God by the natural law in their hearts. Paul seems to connect the natural law with the Mosaic law in Rom 1:32. Paul teaches Jews in Rom 2:13–16 that they are not the only people who have the law, since gentiles also have the law and do it occasionally. For Paul, every mouth is stopped and the whole world is guilty before God, because the law speaks to "those who are in the law," that is, to all human beings. Paul addresses Rom 3:20 not only to Jews but also to gentiles. The failure to be justified by works of the law is not only the Jews' plight but the gentiles' plight as well. Gentiles can be justified by faith in Christ (Rom 3:21–26).

In Galatians, Paul places gentiles under the law as well. "We" in Gal 3:13 refers to gentiles as well as Jews. Paul proclaims to Galatian gentile Christians that they are redeemed from the curse of the law by Christ's sacrificial death on the cross. Gentiles are under the curse of the law because they cannot keep the law perfectly (Gal 3:10). After Christ and faith came, gentiles as well as Jews are no longer under παιδαγωγός (Gal 3:23–24). They are all sons of God in Christ through faith (Gal 3:26). The purpose of Christ's incarnation is to redeem "those who were under the law," that is, gentiles as well as Jews (Gal 4:5). Christ became a human being by being "born of a woman" and being "born under the law" (Gal 4:4).

As a result of our investigation of Paul's understanding of the law and gentiles, we can portray Paul's soteriology for gentiles with enhanced clarity. According to Paul, gentiles are all under sin (Rom 3:9) and under the law

---

2. Räisänen, *Paul and the Law*, 12. Italics original.

3. Räisänen, *Paul and the Law*, 11. See also Stephen Westerholm's summary of Heikki Räisänen's view. Westerholm, *Perspectives Old and New on Paul*, 171–77.

(Rom 3:19, Gal 3:22–24, Gal 4:5). Being under sin is equal to being under law in reality (Rom 5:13–14, 6:14–16; Gal 3:22–23). Anyone who falls short of complete obedience to the law is under the curse of the law (Gal 3:10). Works of the law cannot save gentiles due to the impossibility of perfect obedience to the law (Gal 3:11–12), which is the common plight of human beings. As a solution, God sent forth Christ to redeem not only Jews but also gentiles from the curse of the law (Gal 4:4–5). Christ was accursed for "us" (Jews and gentiles) by being hanged on a tree (Gal 3:13). Participation in Christ by faith makes ours (Jews and gentiles) what Christ did on the cross. His representative and substitutionary death on the cross is for gentiles as well as Jews who are under the wrath of God. In Christ, the blessing of Abraham comes to the gentiles. Receiving the Holy Spirit is the evidence that the gentiles are participants in Abraham's blessing (Gal 3:5, 14). Gentiles who were once held under the law portrayed as παιδαγωγός (Gal 3:23–25) are now sons of God through faith in Christ Jesus (διὰ τῆς πίστεως ἐν Χριστῷ Ἰησοῦ, Gal 3:26). Gentiles who were once under the στοιχεῖα now receive sonship because of Christ's redeeming death for them, who were under the law (Gal 4:3–5). The Spirit crying "Abba, Father" in the hearts of gentiles is the guarantee of the gentiles' sonship (Gal 4:6). In Christ, gentiles are no longer under the law (οὐ γάρ ἐστε ὑπὸ νόμον), which was their existence before the time of Christ. They are now under grace (ὑπὸ χάριν, Rom 6:14). As Timothy George comments, Christ's death on the cross "was not merely another episode in the history of Israel":

> What happened outside the gates of Jerusalem just a few decades before Paul wrote Galatians was not merely another episode in the history of Israel. It was an event of universal human, indeed cosmic, significance. While Paul posed the problem, as he had to, in Jewish terms of blessing and curse, law and faith, it is clear from Abraham on that God's dealings with Israel had paradigmatic meaning for all peoples everywhere. As Paul argued in Rom 1–3, both Jews and Gentiles are 'under the law,' albeit in very different ways . . . Thus the "us" of 3:13—those whom Christ has redeemed from the curse of the law—are not merely Jewish Christians but instead all the children of God, Jews and Gentiles."[4]

After all, who are redeemed from the curse of the law in Paul? It is gentiles as well as Jews, since all human beings are sinners before God because of their failure to keep the law of God, which is manifested in the Mosaic law and the natural law.

4. George, *Galatians*, 233.

Bibliography

Barclay, John M. G. *Jews in the Mediterranean Diaspora: From Alexander to Trajan (323 BCE-117 CE)*. Edinburgh: T & T Clark, 1996.

Barr, James. *Biblical Faith and Natural Theology*. Oxford: Clarendon, 1993.

Barrett, C. K. *A Commentary on the Epistle to the Romans*. HNTC. New York: Harper & Brothers, 1957.

Bassler, Jouette M. *Divine Impartiality: Paul and a Theological Axiom*. Chico, CA: Scholars, 1982.

———. "Divine Impartiality in Paul's Letter to the Romans." *NovT* 26 (1984) 43–58.

Beentjes, Pancratius C. "Some Major Topics in Ben Sira Research." In *"Happy the One Who Meditates on Wisdom" (Sir. 14,20): Collected Essays on the Book of Ben Sira*, 3–16. Leuven: Peeters, 2006.

Bell, Richard H. *No One Seeks for God: An Exegetical and Theological Study of Romans 1.18–3:20*. WUNT 106. Tübingen: Mohr Siebeck, 1998.

Belleville, Linda L. "Under Law: Structural Analysis and the Pauline Concept of Law in Galatians 3:21–4:11." *JSNT* 26 (1986) 53–78.

Bergant, Dianne. *Israel's Wisdom Literature: A Liberation-Critical Reading*. Minneapolis: Fortress, 1997.

Betz, H. D. *Galatians: A Commentary on Paul's Letter to the Churches in Galatia*. Hermeneia. Philadelphia: Fortress, 1979.

Biddle, Mark E. "Baruch." In *The New Oxford Annotated Bible: With the Apocryphal/ Deuterocanonical Books*, edited by Michael D. Coogan. 3rd ed. 176 Apocrypha–183 Apocrypha. New York: Oxford University Press, 2001.

Black, Matthew. *Romans*. 2nd ed. NCBC. Grand Rapids: Eerdmans, 1989.

Blenkinsopp, Joseph. *Wisdom and Law in the Old Testament: The Ordering of Life in Israel and Early Judaism*. Oxford: Oxford University Press, 1995.

Bockmuehl, Markus. *Jewish Law in Gentile Churches: Halakhah and the Beginning of Christian Public Ethics*. Grand Rapids: Baker, 2000.

Boers, Hendrikus. *The Justification of the Gentiles: Paul's Letters to the Galatians and Romans*. Peabody, MA: Hendrickson, 1994.

Borgen, Peder. *Philo of Alexandria: An Exegete for His Time*. Leiden: Brill, 1997.

Bornkamm, Günther. *Studien zu Antike und Urchristentum*. Munich: Chr. Kaiser, 1959.

Bowsher, Herbert. "To Whom Does the Law Speak?: Romans 3:19 and the Works of the Law Debate." *WTJ* 68 (2006) 295–303.

Braswell, Joseph P. "The Blessing of Abraham versus 'the Curse of the Law': Another Look at Gal. 3:10–13." *WTJ* 53 (1991) 73–91.

Bruce, F. F. *The Epistle to the Galatians: A Commentary on the Greek Text*. NIGTC. Grand Rapids: Eerdmans, 1982.

———. *Romans: An Introduction and Commentary*. 2nd ed. TNTC. Downers Grove: IVP Academic, 1985.

Bultmann, Rudolf. *Theology of the New Testament*. 2 vols. New York: Scribner's, 1951, 1955.

Burkes, Shannon. "'Life' Redefined: Wisdom and Law in Fourth Ezra and Second Baruch." *CBQ* 63 (2001) 55–71.

———. *God, Self, and Death: The Shape of Religious Transformation in the Second Temple Period*. Leiden: Brill, 2003.

———. "Wisdom and Law: Choosing Life in Ben Sira and Baruch." *JSJ* 30 (1999) 253–76.

Burton, Ernest De Witt. *A Critical and Exegetical Commentary on the Epistle to the Galatians*. ICC. Edinburgh: T & T Clark, 1921.

Byrne, Brendan. *Romans*. SP, vol. 6. Collegeville, MN: Liturgical, 2007.

Calabi, Francesca. *The Language and the Law of God: Interpretation and Politics in Philo of Alexandria*. Atlanta: Scholars, 1998.

Calvin, John. *Commentaries on the Epistles of Paul to Galatians and Ephesians*. Calvin Commentaries, vol. 21. Edited by David W. Torrance and Thomas F. Torrance. Translated by Ross MacKenzie. Grand Rapids: Baker, 1979.

———. *The Epistle of Paul the Apostle to the Romans and to the Thessalonians*. Calvin's Commentaries, vol. 8. edited by David W. Torrance and Thomas F. Torrance. Translated by Ross MacKenzie. Grand Rapids: Eerdmans, 1960.

Caneday, A. B. "'They Exchanged the Glory of God for the Likeness of an Image': Idolatrous Adam and Israel as Representatives in Paul's Letter to the Romans." *SBJT* 11 (2007) 34–45.

Carson, Donald A. "Why Trust a Cross?: Reflections on Romans 3:21–26." *ERT* 28 (2004) 345–62.

Charlesworth, J. H., ed. *The Old Testament Pseudepigrapha*. 2 vols. New York: Doubleday, 1983–1985.

Clarke, Ernest G. *The Wisdom of Solomon*. Cambridge: Cambridge University Press, 1973.

Coggins, R. J., and M. A. Knibb. *The First and Second Books of Esdras*. CBCNEB. Cambridge: Cambridge University Press, 1979.

Cohen, Naomi G. "The Jewish Dimension of Philo's Judaism: An Elucidation of De Spec. Leg. IV, 132–150." *JJS* 38 (1987) 165–86.

Collins, John J. *Between Athens and Jerusalem: Jewish Identity in the Hellenistic Diaspora*. Grand Rapids: Eerdmans, 2000.

———. *Jewish Wisdom in the Hellenistic Age*. Louisville: Westminster John Knox, 1997.

———. "Natural Theology and Biblical Tradition: The Case of Hellenistic Judaism." *CBQ* 60 (1998) 1–15.

———. "Sibylline Oracles: A New Translation and Introduction," In *Apocalyptic Literature and Testaments*, vol. 1 of *OTP*, edited by James H. Charlesworth, 317–472. New York: Doubleday, 1983.

Coogan, Michael D., ed. *The New Oxford Annotated Bible: With the Apocryphal/Deuterocanonical Books*. 3rd ed. New York: Oxford University Press, 2001.

Cranfield, C. E. B. *A Critical and Exegetical Commentary on the Epistle to the Romans, Vol.1: Introduction and Commentary on Romans 1–8*, ICC. Edinburgh: T & T Clark, 1975.

———. "'The Works of the Law' in the Epistle to the Romans." *JSNT* 43 (1991) 89–101.

Dahl, Nils Alstrup. *Studies in Paul: Theology for the Early Christian Mission.* Minneapolis: Augsburg, 1977.

Dalton, William J. "The Meaning of "We" in Galatians." *ABR* 38 (1990) 33–44.

Das, A. Andrew. *Galatians,* CC. St. Louis: Concordia, 2014.

———. *Paul, the Law, and the Covenant.* Peabody, MA: Hendrickson, 2001.

Davies, Glenn N. *Faith and Obedience in Romans: A Study in Romans 1–4.* JSNTSup 39. Sheffield: JSOT, 1990.

De Boer, Martinus C. *Galatians: A Commentary.* NTL. Louisville: Westminster John Knox, 2011.

DeSilva, David A. *The Letter to the Galatians.* Grand Rapids: Eerdmans, 2018.

Desjardins, Michel. "Law in 2 Baruch and 4 Ezra." *SR* 14 (1985) 25–37.

Donaldson, Terence L. "The 'Curse of the Law' and the Inclusion of the Gentiles: Galatians 3:13–14." *NTS* 32 (1986) 94–112.

Duff, Paul Brooks. "Glory in the Ministry of Death: Gentile Condemnation and Letters of Recommendation in 2 Cor 3:6–18." *NovT* 46 (2004) 313–37.

Dunn, James D. G. *The Epistle to the Galatians.* BNTC. Peabody, MA: Hendrickson, 1993.

———. *The New Perspective on Paul: Collected Essays.* WUNT 185. Tübingen, Germany: Mohr Siebeck, 2005.

———. "The New Perspective on Paul: Whence, What and Whither?" In *The New Perspective on Paul.* 1–97. Rev. ed. Grand Rapids: Eerdmans, 2008.

———. *Romans 1–8.* WBC 38A. Dallas: Word, 1988.

———. *The Theology of Paul the Apostle.* Grand Rapids: Eerdmans, 1998.

———. "Whatever Happened to 'Works of the Law'?" In *The New Perspective on Paul,* 381–94. rev. ed. Grand Rapids: Eerdmans, 2008.

———. "Works of the Law and the Curse of the Law (Galatians 3:10–14)." *NTS* 31 (1985) 523–42.

———. "Yet Once More—'Works of The Law': A Response." *JSNT* 46 (1992) 99–117.

Elgvin, Torleif. "Admonition Texts from Qumran Cave 4." In *Methods of Investigation of the Dead Sea Scrolls and the Khirbet Qumran Site: Present Realities and Future Prospects,* 179–96. New York: The New York Academy of Sciences, 1994.

Elliott, Neil. *The Rhetoric of Romans: Argumentative Constraint and Strategy and Paul's Dialogue with Judaism.* JSNTSup 45. Sheffield: JSOT, 1990.

Evans, Craig A. *Ancient Texts for New Testament Studies: A Guide to the Background Literature.* Peabody, MA: Hendrickson, 2005.

Fitzmyer, Joseph A. *Romans.* AB 33. New York: Doubleday, 1993.

Frid, Bo. "How Does Romans 2.1 Connect to 1.18–32?" *SEÅ* 71 (2006) 109–30.

Fung, Ronald Y. K. *The Epistle to the Galatians.* Grand Rapids: Eerdmans, 1988.

Gaston, L. *Paul and the Torah.* Vancouver: University of British Columbia Press, 1987.

Gathercole, Simon J. "A Law unto Themselves: The Gentiles in Romans 2.14–15 Revisited." *JSNT* 85 (2002) 27–49.

George, Timothy. *Galatians.* NAC 30. Nashville: Broadman & Holman, 1994.

Hansen, G. W. *Abraham in Galatians: Epistolary and Rhetorical Contexts.* JSNTSup 29. Sheffield: Sheffield Academic, 1989.

Harmon, Matthew S. *Galatians.* EBTC. Bellingham, WA: Lexham Academic, 2021.

Harrelson, Walter. "Wisdom Hidden and Revealed according to Baruch (Baruch 3.9–4.4)," In *Priests, Prophets, and Scribes: Essays on the Formation and Heritage of*

Second Temple Judaism in Honour of Joseph Blenkinsopp, edited by Eugene Ulrich et al., 158–71. Sheffield: JSOT, 1992.

Harrington, D. J. "Pseudo-Philo: A New Translation and Introduction." In *Expansions of the "Old Testament" and Legends, Wisdom, and Philosophical Literature, Prayers, Psalms, and Odes, Fragments of Lost Judeo-Hellenistic Works*. OTP 2. Edited by James H. Charlesworth, 297–377. New York: Doubleday, 1985.

Harrison, Everett F. *Romans*. EBC. Edited by Frank E. Gaebelein et al., 1–171. Grand Rapids: Zondervan, 1976.

Hay, David. "Philo of Alexandria." In *The Complexities of Second Temple Judaism*, vol. 1 of *Justification and Variegated Nomism*, edited by D. A. Carson et al., 357–79. Grand Rapids: Baker Academic, 2001.

Hays, Richard B. *The Faith of Jesus Christ: The Narrative Substructure of Galatians 3:1–4:11*. 2nd ed. Grand Rapids: Eerdmans, 2002.

———. *The Letter to the Galatians*. NIB, vol. 11. Nashville: Abingdon, 2000.

———. "Relations Natural and Unnatural: A Response to John Boswell's Exegesis of Romans 1." *JRE* 14 (1986) 184–215.

Helyer, Larry R. *Exploring Jewish Literature of the Second Temple Period: A Guide for New Testament Students*. Downers Grove: InterVarsity, 2002.

Hengel, Martin. *Judaism and Hellenism: Studies in Their Encounter in Palestine during the Early Hellenistic Period*. Translated by John Bowden. 2 vols. London: SCM, 1974.

Hodge, Charles. *A Commentary on Romans*. GSC. Edinburgh: The Banner of Truth Trust, 1983.

Hong, In-Gyu. "Being 'Under the Law' in Galatians." *ERT* 26 (2002) 354–72.

———. *The Law in Galatians*. JSNTSup 81. Sheffield: JSOT, 1993.

Hooker, Morna D. "Adam in Romans 1." *NTS* 6 (1960) 297–306.

Hübner, Hans. *Law in Paul's Thought*. Edinburgh: T. and T. Clark, 1984.

Hultgren, Arland J. *Paul's Letter to the Romans: A Commentary*. Grand Rapids: Eerdmans, 2011.

Huttunen, Nico. *Paul and Epictetus on Law: A Comparison*, LNTS 405. London: T & T Clark, 2009.

Isaac, E. "1 (Ethiopic Apocalypse of) Enoch: A New Translation and Introduction." In *Apocalyptic Literature and Testaments*, OTP 1, edited by James H. Charlesworth, 5–89. New York: Doubleday, 1983.

Jewett, Robert. *Romans*. Hermeneia. Minneapolis: Fortress, 2007.

Josephus, *The New Complete Works of Josephus*. Rev. and exp. ed. Translated by William Whiston. Grand Rapids: Kregel, 1999.

Käsemann, Ernst. *Commentary on Romans*. Translated and edited by Geoffrey W. Bromiley. Grand Rapids: Eerdmans, 1980.

Keck, Leander E. *Romans*. ANTC. Nashville: Abingdon, 2005.

Kim, Hyun-Gwang. "Imitating Christ: An Exegetical Study of Philippians 2:5–11." *AM* 1 (2008) 2–13.

Kim, Seyoon. *Paul and the New Perspective: Second Thoughts on the Origin of Paul's Gospel*. Grand Rapids: Eerdmans, 2002.

Kister, Menahem. "Wisdom Literature and Its Relation to Other Genres: From Ben Sira to Mysteries." In *Sapiential Perspectives: Wisdom Literature in Light of the Dead Sea Scrolls*, edited by John J. Collins et al., 14–47. Leiden: Brill, 2004.

Klein, Günter, "Sündenverständnis und theologia crucis bei Paulus." In *Theologia Crucis-Signum Crucis: Festschrift für Erich Dinkler zum 70. Geburtstag*, edited by Carl Andersen and Günter Klein, 249–82. Tübingen, Germany: J. C. B. Mohr, 1979.

Klijn, A. F. J. "2 (Syriac Apocalypse of) Baruch: A New Translation and Introduction." In *Apocalyptic Literature and Testaments*, OTP 1, 615–52. New York: Doubleday, 1983.

Knowles, Michael P. "Moses, the Law, and the Unity of 4 Ezra." *NovT* 31 (1989) 257–74.

Koester, Helmut. "ΝΟΜΟΣ ΦΥΣΕΩΣ: The Concept of Natural Law in Greek Thought." In *Religions in Antiquity: Essays in Memory of Erwin Ramsdell Goodenough*, edited by Jacob Neusner, 521–41. Leiden: E. J. Brill, 1968.

Kruse, Colin G. *Paul's Letter to the Romans*, PNTC. Grand Rapids: Eerdmans, 2012.

Laato, Timo. *Paul and Judaism: An Anthropological Approach*. Atlanta: Scholars, 1995.

———. "Paul's Anthropological Considerations: Two Problems." In *The Paradoxes of Paul*, vol. 2 of *Justification and Variegated Nomism*, edited by D. A. Carson et al., 343–59. Grand Rapids: Baker Academic, 2004.

Levenson, Jon D. "The Sources of Torah: Psalms 119 and the Modes of Revelation in Second Temple Judaism." In *Ancient Israelite Religion*, edited by Patrick D. Miller et al., 559–74. Philadelphia: Fortress, 1987.

Levison, John R. *Portraits of Adam in Early Judaism: From Sirach to 2 Baruch*. Sheffield: JSOT, 1988.

Longenecker, Bruce W. *Eschatology and the Covenant: A Comparison of 4 Ezra and Romans 1–11*. JSNTSup 57. Sheffield: Sheffield Academic, 1991.

Longenecker, Richard N. *The Epistle to the Romans*. NIGTC. Grand Rapids: Eerdmans, 2016.

———. *Galatians*. WBC 41. Dallas: Word, 1990.

MacKenzie, R. A. F. *Sirach*. Wilmington, DE: Michael Glazier, 1983.

Maertens, Philip. "Une étude de Rm 2.12–16," *NTS* 46 (2000) 504–19.

Marshall, I. Howard. *New Testament Theology*. Downers Grove: InterVarsity, 2004.

Martens, John W. *One God, One Law: Philo of Alexandria on the Mosaic and Greco-Roman Law*. Leiden: Brill Academic, 2003.

———. "Philo and the 'Higher' Law." *SBLSP* 30 (1991) 309–22.

———. "Romans 2:14–16: A Stoic Reading." *NTS* 40 (1994) 55–67.

———. "Unwritten Law in Philo: A Response to Naomi G. Cohen." *JJS* 43 (1992) 38–45.

Martin, Brice L. *Christ and the Law in Paul*. Leiden: Brill, 1989.

Martyn, J. Louis. *Galatians: A New Translation with Introduction and Commentary*. AB 33A. New York: Doubleday, 1997.

Matera, Frank J. *Galatians*. SP 9. Collegeville, MN: Liturgical, 1992.

———. *Romans*, PCNT. Grand Rapids: Baker, 2010.

McKnight, Scott. *Galatians*. NIVAC. Grand Rapids: Zondervan, 1995.

McNamara, Martin, "Some Targum Themes." In *The Complexities of Second Temple Judaism*, vol. 1 of *Justification and Variegated Nomism*, edited by D. A. Carson et al., 303–56. Grand Rapids: Baker Academic, 2001.

Metzger, Bruce M., "The Fourth Book of Ezra: A New Translation and Introduction," In *Apocalyptic Literature and Testaments*, OTP 1, edited by James H. Charlesworth, 517–59. New York: Doubleday, 1983.

Middendorf, Michael P. *Romans 1–8*. CC. St. Louis: Concordia, 2013.

Moo, Douglas J. *The Epistle to the Romans*. NICNT. Grand Rapids: Eerdmans, 1996.

———. *Galatians*. BECNT. Grand Rapids: Baker, 2013.

———. "Israel and Paul in Romans 7.7–12." *NTS* 32 (1986) 122–35.

———. "'Law', 'Works of the Law', and Legalism in Paul." *WTJ* 45 (1983) 73–100.

———. *The Letter to the Romans.* 2nd ed. NICNT. Grand Rapids: Eerdmans, 2018.

Moore, Carey A. *Daniel, Esther, and Jeremiah: The Additions.* Garden City, NY: Doubleday, 1977.

Morris, Leon. *The Epistle to the Romans.* PNTC. Grand Rapids: Eerdmans, 1988.

———. *Galatians: Paul's Charter of Christian Freedom.* Downers Grove: InterVarsity, 1996.

Mounce, Robert H. *Romans.* NAC 27. Nashville: Broadman & Holman, 1995.

Murphy, Frederick J. "Sapiential Elements in the Syriac Apocalypse of Baruch." *JQR* 76 (1986) 311–27.

Murray John. *The Epistle to the Romans: The English Text with Introduction, Exposition, and Notes,* vol.1: *Chapters 1–8.* NICNT. Grand Rapids: Eerdmans, 1959.

Myers, Jacob M. *I and II Esdras.* AB 42. Garden City, NY: Doubleday, 1974.

Najman, Hindy. "The Law of Nature and the Authority of Mosaic Law." *SPhiloA* 11 (1999) 55–73.

Nickelsburg, George W. E. "Bible Rewritten and Expanded," In *Jewish Writings of the Second Temple Period: Apocrypha, Pseudepigrapha, Qumran Sectarian Writings, Philo, Josephus.* The Literature of the Jewish People of the Second Temple and the Talmud 2. Edited by Michael E. Stone, 89-156. Assen, Netherlands: Van Gorcum, 1984.

Novak, David. *Natural Law in Judaism.* Cambridge: Cambridge University Press, 1998.

Oakes, Peter. *Galatians.* PCNT. Grand Rapids: Baker, 2015.

Oepke, Albrecht. *Der Brief des Paulus an die Galater.* THKNT, vol. 9. Berlin: Evangelische Verlagsanstalt, 1973.

Onwuka, Peter Chidolue. *The Law, Redemption and Freedom in Christ: An Exegetical-Theological Study of Galatians 3, 10–14 and Romans 7,1–6.* Rome: Gregorian University Press, 2007.

Osborne, Grant R. *Romans.* IVPNTCS 6. Downers Grove: InterVarsity, 2004.

Peterson, David G. *Romans.* EBTC. Bellingham, WA: Lexham, 2020.

Philo, *On the Creation of the Cosmos according to Moses: Introduction, Translation, and Commentary by David T. Runia.* Leiden: Brill, 2001.

———. *Philo.* Translated by F. H. Colson, vol. 6, LCL 289. Cambridge, MA: Harvard University Press, 1935.

———. *The Works of Philo: Complete and Unabridged.* Translated by C. D. Yonge. Updated ed. Peabody, MA: Hendrickson, 1993.

Polhill, John B. *Paul and His Letters.* Nashville: Broadman & Holman, 1999.

Räisänen, Heikki. *Paul and the Law.* Philadelphia: Fortress, 1986.

Reese, James M. *Hellenistic Influence on the Book of Wisdom and Its Consequences.* Rome: Biblical Institute Press, 1970.

Ridderbos, Herman N. *The Epistle of Paul to the Churches of Galatia: The English Text with Introduction, Exposition and Notes.* NICNT. Grand Rapids: Eerdmans, 1953.

———. *Paul: An Outline of His Theology.* Grand Rapids: Eerdmans, 1975.

Robinson, D. W. B. "The Distinction between Jewish and Gentile Believers in Galatians." *ABR* 13 (1965) 29–48.

Rohde, Joachim. *Der Brief des Paulus an die Galater.* Berlin: Evangelische Verlagsanstalt, 1989.

Rosner, Brian S. *Paul and the Law: Keeping the Commandments of God.* NSBT 31. Downers Grove: InterVarsity, 2013.

Sanders, E. P. *Paul and Palestinian Judaism: A Comparison of Patterns of Religion.* Philadelphia: Fortress, 1977.

———. *Paul, the Law, and the Jewish People.* Philadelphia: Fortress, 1983.

Schnabel, Eckhard J. *Law and Wisdom from Ben Sira to Paul.* Tübingen, Germany: J. C. B. Mohr, 1985.

Schnelle, Udo. *Apostle Paul: His Life and Theology.* Translated by M. Eugene Boring. Grand Rapids: Baker Academic, 2005.

Schreiner, Thomas R. "Did Paul Believe in Justification by Works?: Another Look at Romans 2." *BBR* 3 (1993) 131–58.

———. *Galatians.* ZECNT. Grand Rapids: Zondervan, 2010.

———. "Is Perfect Obedience to the Law Possible? A Re-Examination of Galatians 3:10." *JETS* 27 (1984) 151–60.

———. *The Law and Its Fulfillment: A Pauline Theology of Law.* Grand Rapids: Baker, 1993.

———. "A New Testament Perspective on Homosexuality." *Themelios* 31 (2006) 62–75.

———. *New Testament Theology: Magnifying God in Christ.* Grand Rapids: Baker Academic, 2008.

———. "Paul and Perfect Obedience to the Law: An Evaluation of the View of E. P. Sanders." *WTJ* 47 (1985) 245–78.

———. *Romans.* BECNT. Grand Rapids: Baker Academic, 1998.

———. *Romans,* 2nd ed. BECNT. Grand Rapids: Baker, 2018.

Scott, James M. "'For as Many as Are of Works of the Law Are under a Curse' (Galatians 3:10)." In *Paul and the Scriptures of Israel,* edited by Craig A. Evans and James A. Sanders, 187–221. Sheffield: JSOT, 1993.

Seifrid, Mark A. "Blind Alleys in the Controversy over the Paul of History." *TynBul* 45 (1994) 73–95.

———. *Christ, Our Righteousness: Paul's Theology of Justification.* NSBT 9. Downers Grove: InterVarsity, 2000.

———. "Natural Revelation and the Purpose of the Law in Romans." *TynBul* 49 (1998) 115–29.

———. "Romans." In *Commentary on the New Testament Use of the Old Testament,* edited by G. K. Beale and D. A. Carson, 607–94. Grand Rapids: Baker Academic, 2007.

———. "Unrighteous by Faith: Apostolic Proclamation in Romans 1:18–3:20." In *The Paradoxes of Paul,* vol. 2 of *Justification and Variegated Nomism,* edited by D. A. Carson et al., 105–45. Grand Rapids: Baker Academic, 2004.

Sherwood, Aaron. *Romans: A Structural, Thematic, and Exegetical Commentary.* Bellingham, WA: Lexham, 2020.

Skehan, Patrick W., and Alexander A. Di Lella. *The Wisdom of Ben Sira.* AB 39. New York: Doubleday, 1987.

Snaith, John G. *Ecclesiasticus.* London: Cambridge University Press, 1974.

Sterling, Gregory E. "Was There a Common Ethic in Second Temple Judaism?" In *Sapiential Perspectives: Wisdom Literature in Light of the Dead Sea Scrolls,* edited by John Collins et al., 171–91. Leiden: Brill, 2004.

Stone, Michael Edward. *Fourth Ezra: A Commentary on the Book of Fourth Ezra.* Hermeneia. Minneapolis: Fortress, 1990.

Stott, John R. W. *Romans: God's Good News for the World*. Downers Grove: InterVarsity, 1994.

Stuhlmacher, Peter. *Paul's Letter to the Romans: A Commentary*. Translated by S. J. Hafemann. Louisville: Westminster John Knox, 1994.

Thielman, Frank. *From Plight to Solution: A Jewish Framework to Understanding Paul's View of the Law in Galatians and Romans*. Leiden: Brill, 1989.

———. *The Law and the New Testament: The Question of Continuity*. CNT. New York: Crossroad, 1999.

———. *Paul and the Law: A Contextual Approach*. Downers Grove: InterVarsity, 1994.

———. *Romans*. ZECNT. Grand Rapids: Zondervan, 2018.

———. *Theology of the New Testament*. Grand Rapids: Zondervan, 2005.

Tolmie, D. Francois. *Persuading the Galatians: A Text-Centred Rhetorical Analysis of a Pauline Letter*. WUNT 190. Tübingen, Germany: Mohr Siebeck, 2005.

Van Der Horst, P. W. "Pseudo-Phocylides: A New Translation and Introduction." In *Expansions of the "Old Testament" and Legends, Wisdom and Philosophical Literature, Prayers, Psalms, and Odes, Fragments of Lost Judeo-Hellenistic Works*, vol. 2 of *OTP*, edited by James H. Charlesworth, 265–582. New York: Doubleday, 1985.

VanLandingham, Chris. *Judgment and Justification in Early Judaism and the Apostle Paul*. Peabody, MA: Hendrickson, 2006.

Watson, Francis. *Paul, Judaism, and the Gentiles: Beyond the New Perspective*. Grand Rapids: Eerdmans, 2007.

Weima, Jeffrey A. D. "The Function of the Law in Relation to Sin: An Evaluation of the View of H. Räisänen." *NovT* 32 (1990) 219–35.

Westerholm, Stephen. *Perspectives Old and New on Paul: The "Lutheran" Paul and His Critics*. Grand Rapids: Eerdmans, 2004.

Wilckens, Ulrich. *Der Brief an die Römer*. EKKNT 6.1. Zurich: Neukirchener Verlag, 1978.

———. *Der Brief an die Römer*. EKKNT 6.2. Zurich: Benziger, 1980.

Winston, David. *The Wisdom of Solomon: A New Translation with Introduction and Commentary*. AB 43. New York: Doubleday, 1979.

Wisdom, Jeffrey R. *Blessing for the Nations and the Curse of the Law: Paul's Citation of Genesis and Deuteronomy in Gal 3.8-10*. WUNT 133. Tübingen, Germany: Mohr Siebeck, 2001.

Witherington, Ben III. *Grace in Galatia: A Commentary on Paul's Letter to the Galatians*. Grand Rapids: Eerdmans, 1998.

Witherington, Ben III, with Darlene Hyatt. *Paul's Letter to the Romans: A Socio-Rhetorical Commentary*. Grand Rapids: Eerdmans, 2004.

Wright, J. Edward. "The Social Setting of the Syriac Apocalypse of Baruch." *JSP* 16 (1997) 81–96.

Wright, N. T. *The Climax of the Covenant: Christ and the Law in Pauline Theology*. Edinburgh: T & T Clark, 1991.

———. *The Letter to the Romans: Introduction, Commentary, and Reflections*. NIB 10. Nashville, TN: Abingdon, 2002.

Young, Norman H. "Pronominal Shifts in Paul's Argument to the Galatians." In *Early Christianity, Late Antiquity and Beyond*, vol. 2 of *Ancient History in a Modern University*, edited by T. W. Hillard et al., 205–15. Grand Rapids: Eerdmans, 1998.

———. "Who's Cursed—and Why? (Galatians 3:10-14)." *JBL* 117 (1998) 79–92.

Author Index

Subject Index

Ancient Document Index

APOCRYPHA

Printed in the USA
CPSIA information can be obtained
at www.ICGtesting.com
LVHW060759080823
754344LV00003B/107

9 781666 760569